I0510374

NAU LAB Publishing books may be purchased in bulk at special discounts for sales promotion, corporate gifts, fundraising, or educational purposes. Special edition can also be created to specifications. For details, contact the Publishing Department at stories@naulab.pro

EDITOR'S PREFACE.

I've edited the first two books of the series,
"15 Pictures of the Bar" and "14 Pictures of
the Bench", so after that I expected this one to be of
the same kind – ironic, bitty, sketchy and easy to
read. It proved more serious and even satirical more
than ironic.

I was surprised how involving a reading can be without being adventurous. All my professional life happened in Russian legal field, where jury is not widely
used and is still (though with some "buts", as you will
see in foreword of my legal consultant Russian attorney Alexander Zheleznikov) seen as an element of
new era in law. This book, however, made me rethink
it and made me more skeptical on the matter to say
the least.

The text you are proceeding to is based on a writing
by a renowned and successful attorney and spokes-
men from Chicago Bar of late 19th - early 20 century

Henry Wilcox. The way we read, write and publish has changed phenomenally over the last century. So, I had to rework the text pretty heavily to make it readable, while trying to keep as much of original flare as possible. Sometimes (mostly in the latter part of the book) you will find my comments, quotes and references. Including Shakespeare, of course.

What I have to say, is that however unexpected for a nonfiction book, this one has a twist in the tail that makes spoilers possible. That is why all my references are waiting for you in the pages of "16 Pictures of Jury". I hope you enjoy it as much, as I did.

We are also starting Legal Stories 2.0 series, so I will be astonished to get your comments on different chapters, your anecdotes, sketches, notes and the like. Many of them will then be invited to be a part of this new series. You are welcome to comment on any chapter of any of the three books and mail it to stories@naulab.pro. Legal Stories 1.0 are available on Amazon, and Legal Stories 2.0 are coming.

Margarita Bokshtein
Founding Partner at NAU LAB

LEGAL CONSULTANT PREFACE

Integration of a jury trial always represented for Russian legal reality a new era in life of the society. Being implemented by the great reformer Tsar Alexander Nikolayevich Romanov, the jury trial ran parallel with the abolition of serfdom and (the idea supported by my colleagues) with the introduction of a jury advocacy or "legal profession".

Let us skip the history of the October revolution dark years when the jury trial was abolished, and let's review the situation in the late eighties – early nineties. That was the time when the air was full of numerous and diverse ideas of law enforcement after the USSR collapse. The first post-revolutionary jury trials appeared in 1993, though implementation took ten years in some parts of the country and was accomplished only in 2003.

Process of implementation of this natural for the countries with common (Anglo-Saxon) law institution, was in Russia afflictive, complicated and accompanied with milestone historical events. That makes us wonder about real meaning of jury trial for our country. Most of time Russia and its body politic had no trust in unprofessional court, therefore jury trial primarily seemed a painful extrapolation of its inalienable institutional rights to the population. Indeed, the state idea of the social good which was more important to protect for Tsarist Russian, then Soviet, and then Russian Federation law than personal rights, did not always align with the results of a jury trial. However, history itself clearly demonstrates that a jury trial is the highest, truly democratic form of justice. As a law enforcer, I completely support its wider application and implementation.

Nowadays jury trial is applied not to all types of criminal offenses, and it would be unfair to reproach the state only for this sad fact. I believe that citizens also should be more ready for the role of a judge. Whereas, I often get phone calls from people I know with the same question: "I received a notification I was chosen to be a juryman – how can I dodge it?" Such an attitude to the necessity to sacrifice time and nerves in the name of civic duty is not new for Russia. In the years since reform of Alexander II, wealthy citizens tried to buy off their duty, so the court was actually represented only by the people of property qualification's lower level and therefore was dubbed "court of the paupers". At present, Russian law provides for non-liability in case of evading jury duties. Nevertheless, liability would have disciplined society and made application of this institution much more widespread. Its effectiveness is also evidenced by the percentage of the acquittals, which is ten times higher and keeps growing every year.

In conclusion, the Russian jury trial is on the rise. Let us hope this book will redound to its advantage.

Attorney Alexander Zheleznikov
Founding Partner at Zheleznikov&Partners

CHAPTER I.

Origin and Functions.

That body which we call the petit jury came from remotest times. Tradition says King Alfred gave it birth more than a thousand years ago. Of this there is no record, and the best opinion considers it a Frankish product which followed William into Britain after the Norman Conquest. When Britain's barons wrenched the Magna Charta from King John and formed the firm foundations of the English law, it was provided in that precious charter that none should forfeit life nor lose his freedom or his estates without the judgment of his peers. This clearly meant a jury trial as then existing, and by this act this institution then in use was firmly grafted into English law and came with it across the sea.

When our great fathers shook off the British yoke they still retained the English law, the jury with the rest,

and every state still has the system with slight change. According to the English law, now called the Common Law, the sheriff wrote the names of forty eight free holders of the country where the case was tried in presence of the attorneys on both sides, who each could strike off twelve. the twenty-four remaining made the panel.

Instead of this, in many states statutes have changed the Common Law and names are placed on slips and from a box containing many of these. An officer of court — often the clerk — with bandaged eyes draws out these slips until he fills the panel with the number fixed by law. This varies in the different states, but usually is twenty-four. Then when a case is called, to get a jury for the trial the names of these are placed in some receptacle, from which the clerk or other officer should draw at random, one by one, until twelve are drawn. These make the trial jury.

To be qualified all must reside in that same county where the court is sitting, and there be legal voters. They should not be affined by blood or marriage with either party, nor be older than a certain age. They should have power to read and write, and have no information on the case that causes an unqualified opinion. Each is examined and may be challenged if unqualified, and so excused.

If to many are challenged others may be drawn until the panel is exhausted, and then the sheriff may summon persons standing by to act as jurors. These are known as talesmen, and may be challenged like the others. Most states allow of challenges up to a certain number, for which no cause is shown. When all the challenges are made, the juries are impaneled, composed of twelve, are sworn to try the case on evidence adduced in court and thereon render a true verdict according to the law.

Go to a common court room and see the trial of a case. At one end behind an ornamented desk filling a large upholstered chair you see a careworn, dignified-appearing man. This is the judge, the place he occupies is «the bench».

In front of this a fence is built behind which you find some anxious-looking men and women, who show some evidence of culture. These represent the bar.

Near them a common table stands, on which are books and papers, pens and ink, while seated near are suitors whom they call their clients.

Somewhere about the bench, sometimes in front, but more often at the right, we see another desk, behind which sits an unassuming man. This is the clerk who keeps the files and waits upon the judge; and near him stands a potentate whose majesty sometimes obscures the glory of the bench; this is the bailiff, who speaks short-winded, chopping off his words, while he commands good order in the court.

On one side of the room are placed two tiers of straight-backed chairs. On these we see a dozen people of various types and dressed in different fashions. In cities they may be of different colors and of many nations, some old, some young, some large, some small, most looking weary and demure, twisting and squirming in uneasy seats. These are the jury, and the platform where they sit is called the jury-box. This usually is at the judge's left.

Between the bench and where they sit is placed a chair or stool on which the witness sits in giving evidence. This is the witness-stand.

A few old chairs or benches sit about the room, on which are suitors, witnesses and lookers-on. Somewhere upon the wall an old clock swings its pendulum and drowsily ticks out the time, and in discordant tones strikes out the hours. Anxious care is seen in every face; the air is filled with feverish unrest. This is the stage where human justice holds the scales to measure out the dues of men.

Now note the play that here takes place. The hour arrives at which the court should sit. The judge appears, the people all rise up, the bailiff proclaims the court in session, a case is called for trial, and one by one the jurors called into the box and sworn to answer questions, all challenges are made, the jury sworn to try the ease. The lawyers state each party's claim, the witnesses then testify.

The judge has good facility for taking notes to aid his memory of the evidence. None is provided for the jury. The lawyers often speak, so does the judge, who interrupts with many questions. The jurors are embalmed in silence where they sit like oysters when the tide is out, save as they shift about to ease their bodies on the hard, wood chairs. The judge has been selected for his learning; the jury for their lack of it. He passes on all questions of the law, applies the knowledge that he has and seeks for more. The jury pass on questions as to facts, but can not use the knowledge they possess. Had it been known that they had such knowledge they had not then been chosen.

The nearer their minds approach a blank on questions they must try the better are they qualified. Thus knowledge qualifies the judge, and ignorance the jury. Some jurors never saw a court before; most are bewildered by the strange proceeding and frightened by the pomp and ceremony. They have been captured by the law, taken from their various vocations and brought to court against their will.

Beside the graybeard sits the callow youth, the painter and the peddler, side by side, bookmaker and bookseller near each other, the clerks of banks and carriers of the hod, teamsters and barbers, laborers of the common sort, all confused by stage fright at the part they are made to play.

When all the evidence is in the lawyers on each side address the jury and in most flattering terms dwell on their honesty and intellect. This often is the only point on which the learned lawyers can agree. Each ornaments with virtuous wreaths his client and his witnesses, and paints in darkest hues the vileness of the other side. Each clamoring wildly for a verdict fills the air with lusty shouts for justice.

When all have made their arguments the judge instructs the jury. Sometimes the jury stand while being instructed, straining their ears and minds to understand the words. These instructions are in legal language, containing points often so fine that lawyers scarcely comprehend and the learned judges in the highest courts may not agree upon their meaning. But these instructions are the jury's guide, and must be understood to be effective. They often contain a score or more of legal propositions split in pieces and couched in tangled phrase, ingeniously contrived to give a false impression.

Having been instructed the juries are then locked in a room, the key kept by a bailiff. The room is but poorly furnished, small, and badly aired, where, huddled in a group, sometimes for several days, they spend the long and dreary nights, without a chance to sleep, denied the comforts of the felon in his cell. This is done to force agreement to a verdict, and not until the judge is satisfied they never will agree are they discharged. If they agree, they sign a verdict, return it into court and are released. The judge may render judgment on this verdict or contrary to it, or he can wipe it out and hear the case again. The suit may be appealed, and on appeal the higher court may disregard this verdict and give a judgment to the other side or may remand the case back to the lower court where it is tried again.

Some states make jurors judges of the law in certain cases. Then lawyers read their law books to the jury, who suffer much in hearing what they can not understand. While juries' verdicts sometimes are set aside, usually they are not. Judges prefer to throw on them the burden of decision where they can, and law requires them so to do where evidence is conflicting. Therefore, this verdict in many cases is most important and stands for weal or woe.

They weigh the evidence and measure out the sum and on slight proof may sweep away the savings of a life, or send us to a prison, or the gallows. This is how our dearest rights are placed in their hands. The question of their fitness for this mission is a serious one. Have they the skill to do the work prescribed, and if not, wherein they lack, are questions that I raise herein.

CHAPTER II.

The juror should be honest. No base, unworthy motive should enter in his verdict.

When suits involve large sums the jury may be tempted, and, when not firmly rooted in the path of honor, may yield. The case may then be won by him who has the largest purse.

No legislator yet has found the way to make dishonest jurors honest. Statutes may bristle thick with penal threats as porcupines with quills, and yet the purchase of a verdict be an easy trade when knaves are on the jury. Its members may be herded as if they had a pestilence, or guarded like the prisoners of the state, and yet the expert rascal with the lusty bribe finds secret passage to the outstretched hand. Conscience alone can surely guard the door, and drive away the tempter, and one who has it firmly set needs no protection, but one who doesn't may fall despite all the nation's force hedging about.

Are all the jurors likely to possess this conscience? Are honest men as common that one can seine a dozen when he wishes? Are legal voters of such honest fibre that from a box containing all their names a clerk can blind-folded draw out as many as he wants and never get a scoundrel?

Some legal voters await around the polls from dawn till dark looking for buyers for their votes, with nothing else to sell than these, and sell to both sides if they can. Some pay no debts they can avoid and keep no vows which they can break, and vaunt dishonor as an astute virtue.

Some claim all persons have a price, and he who doesn't get is slow. Some reverence much a finished rascal, regarding crimes well done as noble acts. Will not the names of these be taken from the box?

Where are the merchants selling damaged goods, puffing their sales in scare head ads and offering goods below their cost? Where are those who swindle drunkards in making change, those who sell tickets to the crowd and treat two dollar bills as dollars and with bland, smiling faces claim it a mistake?

Where are the apple vendors who pack the fine fruit in the barrel's ends and put the blasted wind-falls in the middle? And where are the dealers who sell wood and place the knots together, face to face, and thus unduly swell the pile?

Where are the men who sell us spurious gems, adding an oath that each is genuine? Where are the makers of bogus butter, of wine that never knew a grape? Where are the builders who will cover up decayed and shattered stuff with lath and plaster and sell the whole, declaring it without a flaw?

Where are those who bribe conductors to get free passage on the railroad trains and those who hide and skulk and lie to beat their way? Where the conductors that "knock down" fares?

Where are the mining stock promoters? Where are the slick wooers who win a widow to pilfer her estate or steal the heart of some confiding girl to get her fortune?

Where is that numerous army of the vile, gamblers who cheat at cards, bookmakers who fix the races, pickpockets, shell game sharks, thugs, hold-up men and thieves of every kind? To classify them is an endless task. Are not these rascals still at large, their names upon the roll of voters? How can the blinded minion of the law avoid their names when drawing from the box? Will heaven send a loving angel down to guide the hand of him who blinds his eyes? The gods help those who help themselves, 'tis said, and he who blindly trusts to luck, who well might see, can have no claims on heaven.

The clerk who has fair luck will get a just proportion of the vice and fraud held by the box from which he draws. All lawyers trained in jury suits know every jury has such membership in some degree. As types that I have often seen I offer these:

Phil. Floater.

He was a waif of fickle fortune and poor in everything that man may have. His form was lean, loose-jointed, and of bloodless hue, his face of sneakish and frightened aspect. From youth he had been poorly nourished, he ate what he could get, and when, and where it could be got by him, he took the scraps of what was left, after the strong had taken what they wished. Whatever was exposed to theft he took if he could get it without peril. He was the youngest of many children, all reared to forage where they could, picking or pilfering other peoples' crumbs. Phil followed in his father's foot-steps and by an early union had a brood of children who found their education in the street. He hung around saloons, fed on free lunches, looked for a chance to beg a dime; meanwhile his wife did washing to keep away starvation from the home.

He formed acquaintance with small politicians, shadowed their foot-steps and stayed about the places where they met. This way he found employment in odd jobs in politics.

Here he was placed where he could do a kind of dirty work. They so manipulated jury-drawing that they might place him on the jury. This was his harvest field: he many times procured small sums to hang the jury or cause a compromise. Guys like this are often found among the riff-raff of the larger cities, and in some smaller ones. They are the settlings of our social system, who find support in petty pilfering, and any kind of service, good or bad, which they can get to do. The fact that such may sit as jurors and pass upon the legal rights of suitors, reflects upon our legislators and shows how primitive our jury system.

I now give one who started higher but reached as low a level:

Jim Sport.

He sprang from wealthy parents and was early taught the path of honor. He used to have plenty of good books and he had the time to read but was too indolent to struggle up the hill of learning. Pleasure held out her arms. He flew to her embrace.

The soft, sweet dalliance on the lower levels he found more suited to his taste than any of the lofty peaks to which stern virtue pointed. Justice to him was but a name, an empty name contrived to conjure, designed to dazzle fools. However full was the father's purse, when it descended to the sou it soon collapsed with emptiness. He thought it was exhaustless, like an ever-flowing stream fed from unfailing sources, yet found at last 'twas but a lake shut in by narrow limits, kept by the dam his father's patient thrift had raised, and when his unthrift broke the dam away it headlong ran to ruin.

Gambling, the universal vice that curses every nation on the globe and teaches fools to hope from luck and chance the rich rewards which patient toil must earn, quite early caught him. It grew apace till in its feverish trouble he would not hesitate to stake all that he hoped in life upon the throwing of the dice or turning of a card. Often he stood in breathless frenzy straining his eyes to watch the pace of running horses, yelling himself to hoarseness, and hoping the one on which his bet was placed would foremost reach the goal. Then cursing his ill-luck he left the scene and supper less long pondered over his loss, striving to understand how he had been undone. He often lost, yet ever hoped to win upon another bet. Sometimes he did. He cared not what the game, the time, the place, or how great the hazard.

He ever held the hope that by some lucky chance, some trick or underhand device he could succeed and get another's wealth without a just return. Where he had planned to cheat he often was cheated, and knaves much shrewder than himself wrought his undoing. This way he circled downward, aided by other vices, growing worse each day and poorer, changing his gems for gewgaws, his mansion for a single room, where, clad in borrowed raiment, he strove to drive away the wolves of want by any kind of baseness.

So he became a jury fixer and hawked the remnant of his ragged honor to any who would bid. Sometimes he sat upon the jury, wearing the livery of an honest seeming, appeared to listen to the evidence, as if the duty he assumed weighed heavily upon his conscience, when he was planning or had planned, to spend the bribe his perfidy would gain. He was the finished product of that growing vice that blasts the fairest youths in all our land, fills homes, once happy, with its broken hearts, and turns large estates into a stream of waste.

The victims of this vice should not pollute the courts. Their wrecked and wasted lives may well command our pity and inspire a helping hand, but only men who know the face of justice and have walked that path of toil that leads to honor, who gladly offer for what they get its worth in honest service — only those are fit to sit upon a jury.

Here is a juror of another kind and yet as bad:

Walter Whiteslave.

He was the withered remnant of a man who all his life had been a corporation's slave. In infancy he was its errand boy, and rising slowly in his master's service advanced from post to post, and when the weight of years began to bend his form, wrinkle his flesh and spray his head with frost, he held a place which many might desire, yet he was always subject to the will of one above, who at a nod could sprawl him help-less, blacklist him on the roll for like employment, and for-ever shut the door to future earnings in the field where he had spent his life. And so he toiled in fawning attitude and dared not question those who gave him orders. What told to do he did; where sent to go he went; yea, more, he hung upon his master's looks, divined his thoughts and sprang to serve him ere the thought had been expressed in words.

From small beginnings the corporation which he served had grown and spread its tentacles till, like the mighty banyan tree, its roots and limbs extended far, the tender shoots of competition stifled, and had no rivals except those thrifty monarchs of its kind. With these it stood and intertwined its limbs and formed a mighty forest, shutting out the light above and making all a desert in its shade. This corporation was his god, its rules and regulations Holy Writ, its will the voice of law, its friends his friends, its foes his foes, and all alliances which it had formed he counted as his own. As such he sat upon the jury, and there came the poor and weak pleading for justice from such corporations, showing wrongs that cried to heaven for quick redress.

Before him at the bar employed by such defendants he often saw a minion of his master, pride-blouted in its service,

speaking: in tones familiar to his ears. Sometimes his master and the party sued in this way were affined. A great alliance covering half the globe, offensive and defensive, had been formed, and called a pleasant name. In this the master was a member also, linked with it this party to the suit and they with many others acted in concert, like the several parts of one great orchestra.

Could this poor wretch, this aged, labor-crippled slave, with all these odds against him, knowing that a breath of enmity might blow him in the street to starve, look steadily upon the face of justice and with unwavering hand sign a large verdict against his master's friend? Yet he had sworn to be impartial and his high duty to his state and country and the plaintiff he knew full well, but he, who all his life had crept in meek submission to an iron will, which cared not whom it plundered, could not now stand up and show rebellion.

Laws that expect good service from this shackled slave were born in ignorance and should be changed. These truckling servants should never sit on juries. The jury box should be supplied with free men, who know no master but that honest conscience that keeps them ever in the path of duty.

Look at another picture of a common juror, called Thrifty Loeb. Floater was weak as water and was a rascal because he could not help it. Sport was the prey of vice and this tore down the fence of virtue and seared his conscience.

Whiteslave was but a coward weakling, the product of that system which honors power and lets the worthy starve. Now turn to one whose staple vice was meanness, who might have lived an honest and an independent life. He owned a little farm and from its tillage found relief from every pressing want and every day might have become more firm in soul and honor. But he was couched in selfishness as closely as lies the unhatched nestling in the egg, and through its shell he never cared to break. He had no large ambitions, undertook no brilliant scheme of crime, but found his full expression in acts so mean that those who saw them felt less anger than disgust.

Such small positions as the office that supervises roads, or manages the schools, or waits as constable upon a justice court, excited his ambition. They offered him a chance to fleece in some dishonest way the scanty fund a township treasury had gathered. In drawing stealings from so thin a source he showed a genius that if linked with greater force might have made a money magnate of him.

But with his timid wing his flight was low, yet in the region where he worked he missed no opportunity for selfish gain and followed every lead which promised it. Often he got upon the jury and there he sought to trade his verdict for a little pelf. His hand was always out, his eyes were open wide, his sleepless vigil ever was to gather gold or favor by his verdict. His ears were deaf to pleas for justice, his heart was cold to others' wrongs, and that important organ of the

brain which we call conscience was but a wasted membrane
so steeped in selfishness that none could ever wake it.

How to exclude such scoundrels from the jury should be discovered by the legislature. The task is not prodigious. Men of well-proved worth who in the public eye have shown their fitness for exalted trust are not so scarce that we must fill our Courts with such vile trash.

CHAPTER III.

Attention.

A jury box is not a place for sleep, but many try it and succeed quite well.

Others sit half asleep, in mental aberration. Some claim that things told them in slumber are afterwards recalled unconsciously in making up their judgment. This I do not quite believe. The camera takes no photograph without a plate made sensitive. This registers the image. And so the human mind receives no image from objects offered to the eye or ear unless attention is secured.

Some conscious notice must be taken or the event, like all the myriads everywhere occurring, will pass without effect and leave no record in the mind. Some acts compel this notice by their force. But I'm pretty sure the jury must desire to hear the evidence to remember it.

They must give close attention to every word and boar a mental strain from first to last. Can men untrained at listening do this task? Will they be likely to attempt so great a strain? Men of wide learning and ripe experience are quite exhausted by an hour of listening. A lecture, concert, poem, drama, sermon, story, speech, or song running beyond an hour without a rest is likely to be partly lost on worn-out ears. Lectures and sermons mostly are confined to less than sixty minutes. Dramas are divided into acts, each with an interval of rest between.

Why then should jurors be required to rivet their attention for several hours without an intermission. They do not and can not perform the task. Behold them wriggle in their uneasy seats, cross and uncross their legs, look at the ceiling or out on the street, glance slyly at a paper or the clock.

Observe their wandering gaze and note the look of interest come and go as intermittently they think of their affairs, then of the case. The rosy face of that young farmer lad now wears a pleasant smile. Has he untied a knotty problem in the case? Not so; his mind was with the girls down in the orchard beneath the balmy blossoms and the glowing moon.

'Tis cruelty to terminate his dream and make him listen to the evidence. Note on that aged merchant's care-worn face the rising frown. Has he beheld some act or heard some word that causes him to fear a witness has falsely sworn? Not so; he's thinking of his store. His curdled brow is index of the fear he feels that bills maturing while he is on the jury may find no cash to meet them.

That city stripling who looks so pleased is planning for a dance to-night or party at the theater. That fat old man now quite asleep is dreaming it is five o'clock and he's at home. Others are not asleep and yet contrive to while away the weary hours in which a witness cons the items of a long account, by numbering o'er the buttons on his coat, the books upon a table, or noting the peculiar beard or garb of someone looking on.

How to attract attention is a puzzle that advertisers ever find before them. Preachers and actors and all who court the public eye are ever on the rack to solve it. Men will not look or listen long unless they find amusement in so doing or feel compelled to do so by a sense of duty. Great strength must come from training for the purpose for which that strength is used, and power to listen comes from often listening long and well. 'Tis not a bounty from the hand of Nature, but the reward of patient toil.

To show the lack of skill in this regard let me show two sketches:

Calvin Curiosity.

He was born with open eyes and came to see the world. His ears were large and keen to hear, his fingers were long and he greatly enjoyed their use. His mouth was large and filled with ruddy tissues and when he saw a tempting viand it watered with profusion. His health was rugged and he was much alive on every plane. All things of physical or mental nature, or those emotions which pertain to spirit, and every dream and vision that were drawn upon imagination's walls he longed to grasp.

All that a man might wish he sought with strong desire, his heart high-beating longed for every throb of pleasure in the world. He stood upon the loftiest peaks his means could reach. He saw the smallest microbe that his glass could bring to view, he drank all waters and tasted every vintage that he could procure. Rare beers, imported liquors, cordials and mixtures, light and heavy, he eagerly imbibed, not that he wished to drink but only for the knowledge gained thereby.

All foods that man had ever eaten, fowls, animals and insects, worms and beetles, he made familiar, and every fruit, root, vegetable or weed that pleases any appetite he made acquainted with his palate. In his own species, too, he took delight, wanted to meet all men and women, youths and in-

fants, white, black, yellow, red or brown, of every nation, land and tongue. And everything that man has made of art or ornament he wished to view. In this pursuit he would have toured in every land his purse allowed. In the city where he lived he traveled much; center and suburbs and all points between he eagerly explored.

Once only did he use a path if he could find another, moved frequently from flat to house and house to boarding place, changed restaurants and offices and hardly had he made one friend before he left him for another.

The gentle sex of every grade gave him delight. The grave, the gay, the warm, the cold, the stolid, the intense, white, dark, or rosy-tinted, all caused him much amusement for a space. He flitted rapidly from flower to flower and opening bud, nor dallied long enough to make a deep impression. He sought for freaks in men and women and curios everywhere. Music was his delight, but when a song was learned he dropped it from his mind.

The best performers rarely charmed him more than once. And many books he read or scanned. If they were filled with startling stories or pictures drawn in glittering lines, grotesque, or quite uncommon, these he devoured. If they were merely plain but clear and accurate in line and precept he threw them soon aside, abhorring every form of commonplace. He gave attention to religious faiths of his and other lands, and in every creed however strange and difficult, he took deep interest until he knew its salient points, then gave it thought no more.

The pulpit and the rostrum had attraction for him and yet he seldom heard the same man twice, and if at first the speaker dwelt on common things he left straightway and sought another place. And so it was in all his other quests.

He deemed the world a museum to delight his senses, and when his rising wants were satisfied he followed his first impulse that promised a change. This man of eyes and ears and active observations was often seen upon a jury. If the witness' tale was new and told with fervor or dramatic power, he followed it for awhile. If commonplace, or dull, or poorly told, his mind recoiled and wandered to more thrilling subjects, and thus in general he was the worst of jurors. His lack of patience, evident to all, caused lawyers much distress and parties thought that he was set against them. He only saw the tops of facts. His view was like the skimming swallows when flying over a city, who sees a maze of roofs and steeples but has no vision of the life within.

Take an example of another sort: Robert Recluse

He was of a different mould. He, too, had eyes, but they were rarely used except upon familiar things. The common sounds which he had often heard gave him the most delight. He seldom wandered from the beaten path over which his feet trod his whole life. He fastened to the friend who had proved true and never thought of change. He proposed the first love of his youth and wished to live and die with her, and by her side is buried, hoping that they might share immortal life together. In early manhood he had learned a trade under his father's guidance and this he practiced as his father had. He added no improvements and resisted all proposed. The old was good enough for him. His days were filled with steady toil, each day like every other, and the lack of change caused no discomfort.

The few things that he ate and drank were never changed, but in the accustomed order found his palate ever ready to enjoy. He bad about a dozen common thoughts relating to the soul, the future state and social matters, and he often repeated them if he were forced to talk by some occasion, but took the most delight in silence and the peace which comes from shutting out the world. He bent his body to his daily task and there he kept his mind, resisting all attempts to lure it to strange fields and often when invited by words of others he ventured no reply and soon it was clear he had not listened, but was thinking of his work.

Within the narrow sphere in which his life was fixed he was content to know but little. Outside he had no knowledge. Books to him were blanks, the world with all its wealth of wonders to him was as unknown as were the stars, that lighted the pathway on his journey home.

He had no civic pride. He sued no one and none sued him. He asked no favor of the government but to be let alone. He felt a great disgust when he was summoned on a jury. He had no interest in the suits, was not familiar with the language used, disliked the conduct of the court, the advocates and suitors and his fellow jurors, sat under protest, and to what was said and done gave little heed but got away as quickly as he could. He was homo ignoramus of the common type, and yet in one respect was wiser than the men who frame our statutes. He knew he was not suited to the task thus forced on him by law.

I could cite many examples like these. Anyway the two are sufficient to show the need of men for jury service trained to listen, not to amuse themselves but as a duty which the law has laid upon them.

CHAPTER IV.

Perception.

Attention is the photographic plate. Perception is the image formed thereon. Unless the plate is well prepared the image will be blurred, the words be heard and yet not understood, or the motive missed which brought them into being. Thus, to perceive requires a skill which only comes to minds well trained for such a task.

In every suit there is often language strange to those untutored. The law has always had a language of its own. Its words are names of battlefields that fly an unfamiliar flag to eyes untrained. To those instructed in the law, these words have meanings accurate, precise and easy for them to understand.

A barber may possess the greatest skill and mow the stubble from the roughest chin with easy grace, know to a hair just what to cut and what to leave in order that his patron's head may look the best, and he may know the lotion that will coax the straggling fuzz upon the glassy surface of the scalp, persuading it to grow like grass in June. He may draw his razor with an ease and skill matching the master of the violin who glides caressingly his dancing bow across the singing strings. His comb and clippers he may handle well and know the use of every barber's tool, may rub and shampoo, knead and wipe with such rare skill and gentleness that every frowsy, unwashed customer who passes through his hands may issue forth a perfumed pink of beauty and delight. And yet he will easily not understand a fee-tail or a springing use after the judge has told him what they are in legal phrase.

A farmer may reach the top in tilling soil, may know each baneful bug, malicious microbe and devouring. He may recognize each pest that blights and mildews growing crops, may know all kinds of cattle, horses, hogs and sheep that lay or breed with profit, may know the moon and season when to sow and reap, and how to fertilize and trim, and when to sell with largest gains. He may do farmer's work with rarest skill.

He may have trained his body for such tasks until his motions seem a sleight of hand that all may envy, and yet not really mange accurate listening: to the learned judire expound on proof beyond a reasonable doubt and proof to a moral certainty and proof by preponderating evidence. His brain well filled with agricultural lore, lost in bewilderment, may see a mass of many images arise when he hears the court descant upon the difference that exists between a general reputation for a general moral character and such repute for truth or honesty.

The master builder may have the mental grasp to image in his mind a mighty temple and body forth his vision in a form where every part will fit as neatly as the human eye. He may have such skill to manage men that multitudes obey him with delight, and move like armies stirred by martial music led by a great commander; may have a ready use of building art, and all the skill which countless ages have sent down the tide of time, and yet be but a child groping in dark when listening to the judge explain the law of negligence, in forty long instructions setting forth the fine distinctions spun in threads of gossamer, partitions of the thinnest fibre dividing causes immediate and remote, contributing to cause or causing consequential damages.

All these are plain as noon-day to the well-versed lawyer, and easy as the rhymes of "Mother Goose," yet they invite the great mechanic to a realm where all is slippery footing for his untrained feet, and he may wander into many errors unawares.

All this applies with equal force to every adept of the manual arts, not trained in legal phrases, and shows the folly of the law that takes great captains from their chosen fields to make poor jurors of them. If such as these are failures on the jury for lack of legal knowledge, what of the common mass that are thus called to sit? Their minds are merely appetites; they know but little language, and that so poorly that they may stumble trying to understand the plainest words. Some like the Esquimaux could not count ten without great strain and cannot grasp a dozen thoughts and hold them clear. The court's instructions and the law-yer's talk are nebulous to them, the long- drawn trial seems a milky way that paints its path of light across the sky yet leaves the earth in darkness. Jurors may understand the words and get the thought intended by a witness and yet be much deceived because they lack the power to read his hidden motive.

Some have the minds of children and take in all tales well told. They collapse when the stories cross and not compass. Such was the simple mind of

Enoch Good.

His home was near a stream that gently rippled by and nev-er failed. He lived upon his father's farm, its fertile soil gave always some reward, its bubbling springs gushed forth in ever constant streams. The seasons came at their accus-tomed time and brought the birds and flowers that he had yearly seen, since first his infant feet had toddled on the mead. The bees had brought their honey to the hives, from year to year, the orchard its fruitful yield when autumn came, and every plant and tree and clinging vine kept faith with him in blossom and in fruit.

His parents and his friends were ever kind and never had deceived him. Beyond the gentle rising hills that hedged about the cottage where he lived he never cared to roam, the village where he dwelt was all the world he wished to know.

When he became a man the playmate of his youth he made his bride. She was the first to win his love — a cousin on his mother's side — and kept it and never proved untrue.

He voted the ticket that his father voted and read the paper that his father read, at the same church attended, swal-lowed the sermons as young birds their food. His neighbors all seemed true, and he believed them so. He sometimes heard of falsehood as a far-off thing among the most de-praved, but rarely found it in his little world.

This man was drawn upon a jury and was asked to try a case where suit was brought upon a note. The man thus

sued denied he signed the note; two persons swore they saw him sign. He then brought forward four who took the stand and testified they saw him pay the note in full.

How could this guileless, simple-minded man to whom such falsehood was unknown unravel such a tangled skein and draw the thread of truth? Lawsuits are born of falsehood. The truth is rarely told by all the parties, sometimes both deal in lies. They come to court with their well-varnished tales, trained and much practiced, and with a skill that would adorn a better cause they act the part of martyrs to the truth.

The untrained, inexperienced novice who does not know the color of a lie can find no explanation to the puzzle, and in his efforts will often push aside the solid gold of truth and choose the plated ware. Fraud comes to court dressed like the truth and wears its mask so well that the unpracticed juror believes it guiltless. The numerous holes which penetrate her mask are smaller than juror's eyes can see; the places where her garments fail to fit escape his notice. The times fraud over-plays the part of innocence by puffing it too much he does not note. All these indices of guilt she hides are patent to a well-trained judge. For many years true and false have passed before his eyes making their claims for his redress. He knows the gait of each, the ring of truth and falsehood, and as the case proceeds shrewdly divines the purpose held by

each party to the suit, the feeling of each witness, and remembers all when making up his judgment.

Such men as Enoch Good, who have no knowledge of the guile that enters in such suits, are no more fitted to ferret out the facts from such a mass of lies than are the lap-dogs fondled at the hearth suited for hunting foxes in the tangled woods.

CHAPTER V.

Memory.

An accurate image may be lost when memory is bad. The imprint which a fact has made upon the mind may be so faint that what occurs thereafter wipes it out. A judge takes notes of all the evidence to aid his memory and sometimes has a transcript furnished to him. Trained even as he is his memory often fails and much he needs this aid. The juries have no training and no means of taking notes, nor are they furnished any transcript but are supposed to carry all the evidence in mind, the rulings of the judge thereon and how each witness did appear when on the stand. Some trials last for many weeks and scores of witnesses give evidence. All this the jury must remember till they reach a verdict, or its effect is lost.

Have jurors such colossal minds that they can grasp this vast array of facts and hold them till they reach the jury-room? They are not really equipped like this. Plagued by unfamiliar words, stage frightened by their queer position and filled with worry of their own affairs now needing their return, they are confused and get but faint impressions of the matters taking place, and have at best but hazy notions of what has occurred. Some of the leading points they may recall but all between is vagueness or a blank.

Lawyers who know the witness well have heard him tell his story and written down his tale, often can not recall his evidence when needed in their argument. Then how absurd to think a jury with so poor a chance could excel the skillful advocate. Few persons realize how little they recall of that which has oc-curred the day before. Some hear a lecture and forget the subject, a sermon and can not recall the text, or read a book yet can not quote a line without substan-tial error. The juries are but average men with com-mon faults that mark us all and few can realize how little they recall about the cause when they have reached the jury room.

That which they heard the last will have most force and statements made by fellow jurors assuming to recollect what they do not will have great weight.

Bad memories are of many kinds. Some may remember names and yet not faces, others recall the face but not the name. Some may bring back the place with ease, while they can not tell the things that occurred there. Dates sometimes are impressed upon the brain of those who have but faint impressions of other subjects, while many who can not remember dates are good recalling other things.

Between the best and worst of memories are many grades, but there are very few who can remember all things well. We can recall with greatest ease the things we most desired to hear and fully understood, but things we did not wish to listen to and had no clear perception of we rarely can recall. The poorest memory may be trained to give good service, and the best one may by lack of care become the worst. Bad specimens appear on every jury, and here are two not of the worst:

Benjamin Bookworm.

His chief delight was books. From infancy the lettered page was more to him than all beside. This appetite increased with years, until he hungered to devour all forms of reading matter that the world contained. Nor was he careful what the matter was, if he found it printed, except perhaps the older and more fanciful the tale the greater did he relish it.

Statistics and chronologies, records of births and deaths of ancient kings, and genealogies from tombs deciphered, the dates of battles fought so long ago that nothing but records of the dates and names remained upon the mouldering monuments, all of these filled his soul with ecstasy when head in musty books, but whether his characters lived or died he did not care to hear, but rather thought the time was wasted which was spent in hearing of the joys or woes of men he knew.

Even these if found in print he took sonic interest in, and yet had not the flavor of delight which came from subjects more remote when found between the lids of ancient books. With time some events became prodigious, and the most commonplace affair when long corroded with the rust of time became a precious morsel.

The silly doings of a petty prince, the gibberings of a naked savage, the antics of a bug, an ant, or worm, bivalve, or microbe, when told in printed letters, had more of interest to him than did the sight of many thousand men moving in solid phalanx to fence the country of his birth against invasion. For many years he lived so near a mighty waterfall, that he could hear its roar, yet went not out to see it, meanwhile he conned with eagerness prolix accounts of many distant cataracts, such as the Nile, or Wirmepeg.

He dug for things that time had buried deep, delved for the roots of long forgotten tongues and felt the greatest glee when he could see how sand or sandstones had contained the crumbling bones or fossilized remains of creatures now extinct.

His form was frail and poorly nourished. His pale blue eyes were overhung with shaggy brows. His head topped like a mountain peak above the timber line, where trees and furze and mountain grass yielded at last to barrenness. His long nose ended in a downward turn. His chin was thin and pointed. His eyes worn out by poring over books were almost blind and only by strong glasses could be made to see. He learned to skim from page to page and book to book with rapid speed, not seeking to retain for full use of the matter that he read.

The images gained this way were soon erased by many that displaced them, and these in turn were blotted out by others that succeeded. His memory thus became so bad that he could scarce recall the number of his home or tell his children's names, and more than once he did forget his own, but this was when exhausted, and his mind distraught by weariness.

He had repute for learning, and when not worn out by most prodigious reading he could recall the births and deaths of many ancient kings and salient facts upon a host of subjects, and what he did recall was quite exact and not the product of his erring fancy.

When he was called to jury duty he was much disgusted. He hated courts that forced him from his books and made him hear of things that he disliked. His mind recoiled from these and turned to other things, preferring foreign lore to native facts. The intervals between the sittings of the court he spent in efforts to regain the time thus taken from his books, and when at last the case was tried, the arguments and court instructions heard, like some poor captive to a dungeon scourged he went with fellow jurors to the jury-room. Unfortunately, there, when he strove to recall the stories that had been told him from the witness stand, he found his mind was blank, except on some most striking points, and this he had to fill with what his fellow jurors claimed to recollect.

Lucius Quintius Curtius Loquacity.

His head was large, his hair was coarse and plentiful, and black as jet, his skin was dark and leathery, his eyes wide open and of darkest hue, his neck was thick and short and stiffly held his square, strong jaws and head upon his massive shoulders, his beard was bristly and stood about his large, coarse mouth and heavy teeth like hazel stubble round a rocky chasm.

He was a fountain of vociferation that drew its water from an inner source and promised great abundance. Few were the books or papers that he read, and these he read in haste, and always was he bored when others read what they admired to him.

Silence he much despised and more than that disliked to remain in silence while others talked. He wished no gift of information or advice. In this he most desired to be the giver and he made such gifts with reckless prodigality even to those who least desired them. His lungs were large and strong, and well supplied an active throat and tongue with air to keep them moving. These he could start and then leave or go to sleep, so far as mental effort was concerned, and they would run for hours with greatest speed and never drop a stitch or show the least respect for any who would interrupt. The product was a mass of stuff, stale and most commonplace, chop logic and wretched sophistry mixed with false statements that bubbled upward from within like emanations from a putrid pool.

His rich imagination was a bank that never closed its doors or had occasion to reject an overdraft. On this he scattered checks like flying leaves when Autumn's gusts are whistling through the woods. Sometimes he hit upon a fact, but this he painted with a hue so strange that it misled instead of guided. All things which effervesced so freely were uttered with such force that calling them in question seemed like a challenge to a mortal combat. Few cared to contradict his furious words or try to modify the stand he took.

This man was often foreman of the jury, and there his brutal presence had great weight. As boys cut twigs from saplings and bend for bows or hoops or any form they like, so he did turn and twist his weak-willed fellow jurors to sign the verdict that his will dictated. As a result he who gave but slight attention to the trial and heard but little and less understood, and what he heard had mostly misremembered, now forced his highly-colored fancies on his fellow jurors and wrote their verdict for them.

CHAPTER VI.

Suspending Judgment.

The mob makes quick decisions. A rumor may raise a lynching party. A falsehood which some reckless hand has put in print may light the fagot without any proof. The public acts on first impression and rarely stops to hear both sides. But those who sit in judgment should wait with patience till all the facts are in.

Suspending the judgment needs much training. A lawyer learns it in preparing cases, but its perfection only comes through long judicial service. That jurors should possess this power all must agree, but few, indeed, are thus equipped. Most reach conclusions in advance from lawyers' statements or testimony first presented. Such minds are traps that spring before the game is underneath, are guns discharged half-cocked, fireworks that flash and fizzle in the crowd. They reach conclusions on slight evidence and hold them with a dogged force.

To their set minds all facts against their fixed opinion are much unwelcome and treated as aspersions. Most dread suspension of their judgments, for such sus-jiension is a painful state which they lack patience to endure. They have no ease till they have taken sides and donned the armor which it wears, and this is true of jurors. Their lives are spent in occupations where they decide in haste, acting on general knowledge or mere intuition, on any plan or question, not waiting to gather all the facts or taking pains to weigh them.

Business men have been considered ideal jurors and courts are pleased to get them when they can. To hold them on the panel is not easy, so numerous and pressing their excuses, and when they sit it is against their wills. They constantly complain that they are losing much while thus on duty, show great impatience with the judge and all who take part in the trial, alleging lack of speed and foolish practice in the court, and clamoring to get away. Take now a few examples of our business men and see if they arc fit for jury service.

Rush Hurryman.

His father died soon after he was born, leaving a little suburban notion store and many debts he could not pay. His mother took the assets and her sad condition checked to some extent the pressing claims of creditors. They showed her mercy and she carried on the business of the store, paying in small installments a portion of the debts. She worked like this for years, earning a meager living for herself and son.

Almost as soon as he could talk the boy became his mother's clerk. Here did he show such talent that it soon appeared that he was formed for sale and barter. Quick to detect the wants and whims of buyers, inspired to say the word that stimulated trade, he showed much skill to reach the buyer's purse. He knew how large a price could be obtained, whom he could safely trust, and just the moment when to push the goods upon the buyer. This did he learn to do with such adroitness and sweet, winning ways that the hesitating buyer felt it sin to doubt the seller's faith or fairness of the price.

What learning he acquired he got about the counter in his store, and contact with his customers and those from whom he bought. When to buy and what and when and how to sell and get the highest price, these were his quest and made his world of knowledge. This he acquired so rapidly and used with so much skill that long before his manhood had been reached the legacy of debts his father left was fully paid and the little notion store expanded to a general one where every kind of goods were kept.

The suburb where he lived increased in population and most of it he knew; with his increasing means his fame increased and many saw his rising power and prophesied a brilliant future. "When he had reached the age of twenty-one an offer came that took him to a central point. The owner of a larger store weighed down with years desired a younger man as partner in his business, and of all he knew this thrifty boy appeared to him the best. This offer he embraced, became a member of the combination formed, proved worthy of the trust imposed, mastered so soon its intricate affairs that its large business came to his control and he assumed a pedestal from which he viewed the world of trade and had his finger on its market's pulse.

Quicker and farther than all competitors his bright eyes saw and intellect discerned. His little and agile body, nimble as his mind, overmatched his slow opponents. Numbers that told of profit and of loss he quickly read and at a glance absorbed the gist of that affecting his affairs. With telescopic vision he beheld the mountain peaks that commerce reared in lands remote and was the first to see the storm clouds threatening to destroy, and note the place where they would likely break.

He rarely bought too much, but when he did and saw a loss impend he quickly turned, cut short his loss and let his prof-

it run. One by one his rivals bit the bitter crust of ruin, their wares were sacrificed and he became the buyer. Their wrecks he made his glorious wreaths. As they fell down he rose and grasped a wider field of trade, waxed in riches and in power, and where a thousand common merchants thrived but few remained.

These were mammoths of colossal wealth- and he was one. These still were his competitors until he shrewdly struck the master stroke that blended all in one immense combine. This placed him at its head. Here from a central point for many years he held a thousand reins, guiding many fiery steeds all bent with haste for gain. He toiled like this until with age his flesh was shriveled to the bone by anxious care, his mouth was puckered like a miser's purse, his features pallid as the face of wan distress, and yet he moved like lightning, excelling all in mental speed and quick resolve. This man was caught while in the hottest fever of his mighty strife for gain and made to sit upon a jury.

There he was asked to try a case wherein the question was, who owned a certain brindle calf. Would he sit calmly through the summer days, dismiss the business of his mammoth store, confine his mind to note the long description of this calf and of the one that had been lost? Would he with care collect descriptive points from all the witnesses who testified tending to show resemblance or dissemblance in the calf, giving to each due weight, and from the whole, enlightened by the lawyer's argument and instructions of the court, give to the quest a sober, careful, and deliberate judgment, forthcoming only after all had been considered?

I am certain he would not. He would regard the question as a trifle, mooted by fools, not worth his serious thought. He would decide it quickly and turn away as if it were a nuisance which courts and lawyers bred for their own gain. That puts him out of his proper place and no more fit for court affairs than lawyers for his store.

The world of commerce is a den of beasts with claws and teeth to tear down and devour. Those best succeed who are most agile, and to their strength add speed. Look at that broker dancing to the ticker. His ears are quick to hear its tale that may mean wealth or ruin. Behold him tread on air when he succeeds, or see him drag his lifeless limbs when withered by defeat.

Now up, now down, then up again, swings the swift pendulum of his fickle fortune from day to day until at last death calls his turn, his option closed, and drags him from the floor as a mass of shattered nerves and wasted sinews. His faded eyes in frenzy roll as he in faltering accents begs a chance to place a further margin. Since first in youth his frail bark met the billows that surged so wildly on the speculative sea, his every nerve has strained with utmost tension to grasp the goal of wealth.

Days in hot haste followed by nights of fever, uneasy tumbling on a sleepless pillow he plotted eagerly to win, and

fondly counted his expected gains. His life is but a battle wherein minutes may fix the fate of years and speed alone may bestow the prize. Can such a character sit on a petit jury and listen with patience to a quarrel about a cow? Can he with care and neatness piece together the scraps and fragments of each story told, until in one clear garment of unsullied truth the whole may glow in radiance and perfection? Such seems to me unlikely. With deep disgust his mind would surely wander far from the case and curse the luck which gave him such a task. Before the evidence was closed or any witness had been sworn he would be ready with his judgment of blame for one or both.

Turn from this broker to another juror whose lifework lies in quite a different field. Behold the prince of butchers whose keen knife lets lifeblood daily from a myriad swine. Sturdy he stands, stained to the waist in gore, grasping his blade for no unsteady stroke. Not great Achilles on the field of Troy piling the gory ground with heroes slain has shed more blood than he draws in a day. Quick as a flash his trained eye notes the vein, his strong arm swiftly guides the unerring steel and draws it forth again so suddenly that the spurting blood scarce strikes it ere it finds another place in its next victim's throat. He deals with death daily with greatest speed and grace of motion and his struggling captives have scarcely time to shriek before their lives have fled. And well he may be active, for many thousands wait along the line to finish the products of his hands. His keen knife forms a most important link between the pigsty and the royal spit, and millions scattered over all the globe are eager for the finished product.

Would this rare genius of the packing plant who looks and strikes as quickly as he looks be fitted for the jury? Would he suspend his judgment or keep his mind from forming a conclusion till all the facts and reasons are presented?

Take then the music master, who dreams cadences and arpeggios and hangs his hopes of wealth and ease on sweet caressing sounds. Behold him tear his uncropped locks in furious rage or seize his awkward student's instrument and smash it on the luckless urchin's head because forsooth he has unwittingly mixed discord with the velvet symphony. Would such as he be likely to sustain suspended judgment through the many days of trial?

Then take the pampered pets of overloaded wealth whose highest cares converge and center in the color of a tie, the creasing of a pair of pantaloons or the denouement of a chance flirtation. Are these the kind who holds their minds at bay until the time is ripe for forming judgment? If these the generals in the field of action and these the darlings in the homes of plenty have not the poise and patience to suspend their judgment until the proper time, what of the privates in industrial armies?

What of the ragged wretches whipped by fortune? Can those who see the almshouse or a prison the only haven of life's dreary winter, and like the worn-out swimmer still must buffet against the tide, can such be calm and steady combining from day to day with care the sheaves of evidence, loading each in its appropriate place and keep the load intact till taken to the room where it is threshed and winnowed and the grains of truth extracted from the straw and chaff?

Habits of thought are not abandoned in a day because a judge requests it. The mind is a machine nicely adjusted and set for certain actions, which it will have or none. The passing years have put the parts in place, set cogs and shafting and the belts thereon, and fixed the speed and ends to while it moves, and when some unskilled engineer mistakes its nature and puts it to a different task he soon discovers in the poor results the proof of his perversion.

Machines designed for shaping spikes can not be used to sharpen needles, and minds so unaccustomed to deliberate action are not adapted for judicial duty.

CHAPTER VII.

Bias.

Bias in countless ways brings misery to the human race. All annals of mankind reveal its havoc. The stories of its crimes blot every page. It plunges nations into war, rends empires with secession, and often makes the state a hotbed of rebellion. It organizes every mob that bids defiance to the law. Inhuman cruelty with the help of bias becomes delight. It fastens to the cross and stake the purest and most loving' hearts. It spreads its poison in society of every rank, depletes success in every branch of man's affairs, and strikes at every institution of the state, but nowhere has it greater power to harm than in the courts.

A most pernicious form abounds in many jurors. They yearn to help the weak against the strong. This kind of bias is seldom disclosed before it is too late, for those who have it swear they have it not, and protest strongly in their oaths that no amount of crying need or claims of sympathy can swerve their judgment in the least degree.

All this they may believe, yet, when the crucial test is made, and they see crippled innocence oppressed with want, praying relief against defendants armed with wealth, they cannot stay the sympathetic hand, and thus the rich man finds his wealth against him weighed.

The adult by the infant is outweighed, a woman's rights made greater than a man's, and poverty soon tips the beam when corporate wealth sits on the other scale. All will admit that neither youth nor age, sex, wealth nor health nor any kind of status should move the scale a fraction of a hair when justice weighs the facts before the law. But what does a sympathetic jury care for this?

Their heart throbs stifle reason's voice while they divide the gifts by fortune made and make the rich disgorge to feed the poor, the strong to help the weak, the sterner sex to bear the weaker's load. They despoil defendants, and make the court an almshouse for the poor. Most men are tender toward the needy and much inclined to aid them. This kindness should appear in acts and gifts made by each person on his own account, from his own means, not taken under color of the law pretending payment of a debt where none exists.

Despoiling another of his means is confiscation and should be classed as such. Few are the jurors who have not this fault in some degree. They lack that clear perception which should restrain the promptings of the heart, and thus they fall an easy prey to such appeals as lawyers make to stir their blood.

Let us note another kind of bias: the sort inspired by certain kinds of suits. Sometimes a claim is quite distasteful to the jury because the law which gives the right is not approved, and they refuse to grant relief save on the strongest proof. Sometimes they so abhor the crime that has been charged that they will raise the sword to strike upon a mere suspicion, and then the accused cannot escape their wrath except by clearest proof of innocence.

Most will agree, that the bias such as this is the most unjust. The matter in dispute should not affect the law, nor change the measure of the evidence required to prove a fact. A bushel should be the same in size of any substance measured, a gallon should contain four quarts same of soda or champagne.

Most jurors can not comprehend this simple truth and so stretch their arms to jerk one culprit from the jail and push with eager zeal another in, they pass upon the wisdom of the law and if they find it faulty, set the captive free. If they approve, they gladly give it force. When some vile crime arouses public rage, they take the first suspected as an object lesson and if he cannot show an alibi in proof so clear that none can find the spot to place suspicion on, they seize him in the whirlwind of their wrath and send him to the gallows.

When excited so much by a thirst for blood, the average jury then becomes a mob, and a jury trial but a lynching party, conducted with some order. They sense the feelings in the air, and recognize no curbs to make them wait for proof. The court's instructions are but paper wads blown from uncertain guns which make some noise but always miss the mark, unless they tell the jury to acquit.

While bias follows general lines, 'tis subject to no certain rules. Most lean in favor of a damage claim when brought by injured persons, but some are strongly set against such suits. Many dislike the liquor laws and strive against convictions under them, and others loathe the traffic with so great a hate that they convict upon the slightest proof. A common gamester shields the gambling den and bends the bars to let its boss escape. The brothel's patron lets its inmates go, yet there are some who patronize each place that go against the facts to punish those accused of either crime.

Bias may spring from politics or any social status, may have religion for its fountain head, or learning as the object of its hate. The ignorant despise the learned and when a doctor or a lawyer sues for fees, oppose the payment of his legal claim and slice the sum and thus appease their bias.

So various are the kinds of bias that find a lodgment in the minds of jurors that listing them becomes too great a task. Take two examples of the common kind quite often seen.

Anthony Saint.

His form was tall and slender, his nose was long, his hair was coarse and straight. He wore it long and usually unkempt, his beard was patriarchal and both hair and beard were thin and of iron gray, resembling much the whiskers of a goat. His cheeks were sunken, his forehead thin and high, his eyes pale blue, set under bushy brows, which bore the traces of a constant frown. His temperature was cold, complexion pale, his garments plain and misfits of the coarsest kind. He stood erect, straight as a pine and walked with firm, defiant tread. He had descended from the loins of toil, a line of men inured to the hardest kind of manual tasks. He was a self-made man of which he was most proud, he scorned all shams, despised the hypocrite, and looked on learning with contempt.

Prompt and exact in all his deals he often walked the floor late in the night for fear he could not meet a bill maturing on the morrow. So anxious was he to be fair and true, and keep above reproach, that he gave many more than was their due. And yet suspected every other man and found in all some fault that he disliked.

He understood, obeyed, yet formed no union with any church, because he found no creed he could endorse. In politics Anthony Saint was independent, voting, with pride, for those who had no chance to win. He deemed his country's institutions wrong, and felt himself inspired to urge a change in laws and their enforcement, and so from crown to toe was filled with strongest bias, yet was he sure that everyone was wrong except himself and he the only fair, unbiased person in the land.

He was sometimes compelled to sit upon a jury. Here he considered courts were bad inventions, contrived by lazy and dishonest lawyers to take advantage of the simple minded.

He held all controversies should be settled out of court, where some fair man (such as himself) should be the chosen arbiter, and so was opposed to every suit and every one who brought it into court.

A slight suspicion raised against a woman made him discredit her whole story. No spectacle of sorrow touched his heart or softened his austerity, and those who sought to move him by a show of anguish caused him to turn against them. He would not listen to the lawyers' talk, assuming he knew more than they, nor did he heed instructions from the judge. The law he claimed was common sense, and this he thought he had. When the jury had retired he stated what the verdict ought to be, assuring all that he would sign no other. He said but few words and then maintained a sullen silence. His fellow jurors plead with him for hours and sometimes days seeking to compromise upon a verdict, but found the effort vain, and either the others came to him or else there was no verdict.

Note now a juror of a different type.

Barney Blubber.

He was short and fat and round in all his features, his face smooth shaven and his hair clipped closely to the scalp, his short, fat neck as ruddy as his full red cheeks, his eyes were large and watery, his eye brows arched, nose thick, lips large, chin full and deeply dimpled. He was on good terms with the world and all its pleasures on the common plane were suited to his taste.

Speculations on the future state were naught to him. He didn't puzzle his brain with metaphysic thoughts. He championed no reforms, was fitted to the world as it now is, and wished to see no change. He was not moved by scruples or the claims of persons or the public, his heart was large, his hand was warm, his friends were many, and to their wants he gave a quick response.

When on the jury he showed his feelings for an injured plaintiff who sued for damage against the rich, the last speech always caught his fancy — such the advantage that the plaintiff' had. He scarcely could restrain his tears when sorrows were depicted and his sympathetic eye inspired the plaintiff's advocate to make a moving plea. But when the case was criminal, involving life or liberty, he was against the state, and favored an acquittal unless the charge was one of great atrocity and then the victim of the crime might have his sympathy and cause him to convict.

He was a child of impulse with no certain sense of right, and seldom the first opinion he had formed would last until the end. Some other juror of a firmer sort with a persuasive voice could swap him from his moorings by statements not in evidence, and make him sign a different verdict from the one which he had planned.

Nor was he strong to stand against attack. He cowed before the threatening attitude of those who would browbeat or use coercion, and when the larger number took a different course than his opinion pointed, he changed reluctantly, and followed them rather than to disagree, accepted that which he had first opposed. He thus gave up his sympathies and left the path of duty to carry favors from his fellow jurors.

Such men are often found upon a jury; sometimes they make a large majority and often all the jury, and then the last speech gets the verdict, unless the other side has much the larger claim for sympathy. Where such a man as Saint is mixed with Barney Blubber, he writes the verdict, if one is reached. Between these two extremes are many grades, some filled with bias when they take their seats, some ready to imbibe it as a thirsty sponge, and others weak as water to its influence.

The slightest trifle often wins the ease, a circumstance light as the thinnest gas that appears in the air, will often in such minds have greater weight than reams of evidence read in depositions or solemn asseverations made from the witness stand by those whose characters are unassailed.

A smile, a smirk, a handshake from a lawyer in the case calling the juror by his given name as in familiar friendship, a chance resemblance to a relative, a residence at the juror's native town, voting his ticket, attending the same

church, matters which have no bearing on the points in is-sue, possess great weight in making up a verdict. These facts are known to lawyers and thus they bow and fawn, hoping to win the juror's favor or counteract the bias inspired by courtly conduct on the other side.

Where the cause espoused gives chance to sue for pity or awaken rage, they beg for tears in tones like mourning doves, or call for vengeance like an angry god. In this way a jury trial has become uncertain as a game of chance, defy-ing all predictions and in its conduct oft is so absurd that did not life and liberty depend thereon, it would become a mark for laughter or contempt. The men who sit in judg-ment on their fellow men should tower above these petty things, and see beyond the mists that bias has upraised the fair, unclouded face of justice, as formed and finished by the law and facts.

CHAPTER VIII.

Judging.

We enter now the precincts of that room in which the jury gather to consult. This is the sacred sanctum, where blind justice secretly sits to weigh all matters with her even-handed scales. Each juror now becomes a judge of high prerogative. From out the many chambers of his mind he must bring out the facts in evidence, the rulings of the court and see in memory again the witnesses who told their stories to him from the stand. He must recall their motions and their manner, the tone and texture of their emanations and every sign and symptom that give the stamp of truth or falsehood to their tales.

Like two proud champions set against each other in knightly lists for mortal combat, he should arrange and place the facts which fight on either side, observe all points of strength, and note all blemishes, find every hole or weakened joint disclosed in cither's armor, and watching closely the minutest motion and hearing quickly the faintest word, decide which champion is the knight of truth and which is the pretender.

His eyes must be familiar with the face of truth that he may recognize her at a glance. His ears must know the tone in which she speaks that he may not mistake her words.

A botanist when shown a leaf tells accurately the tree on which it grew. A judge familiar with the ways of witnesses can easily detect the nature of a tale. All matters move in perfect order; causes connect effects in natural sequence, and make a perfect chain which has no missing link.

Feelings and even thoughts are causes, each having an effect of its own nature, and he who sees all clearly reads the motive in the act. The true tale has foliage differing from the false. Its roots run deeper and its branches wider spread; its fruit a sweeter flavor to the taste, and looks much finer when examined closely. All products manufactured for the occasion begin and end too soon and lack fitness with surrounding facts.

A lie is like a patch which some shrewd tailor places on a garment. It seems to fit so perfectly, that the unpracticed eye detects it not, but every tailor sees it at a glance. A perjured story is a counterfeit which long may pass unchallenged by those unskilled in detecting it, but when it meets the practiced eye, its baseness is at once observed.

As writing experts tell the note that's forged, so expert judges find the tale that's false. A man must save his time in every field where he becomes an expert, and training in one trade will not suffice for others. Some show great skill in guessing weight of cattle, who could not estimate a load of hay and tell its weight within a hundred pounds. No one is born with wisdom. In every calling all must it acquire by trudging up the stony hill of hard experience. This is the only way to reach the lofty heights.

Weighing evidence and detecting truth are no exceptions. Some say that truth is in a well. If this is so, who draws her forth must learn to dive. In litigation truth is often hiden beneath a mass of many falsehoods and fair seeming, and he who want to uncover it must learn to dig.

The task of picking out the truthful tale is not so easy as it seems, but it is the pastime of a summer afternoon compared with that much greater task which every juror should perform. He must apply this truth when ascertained to all the complicated questions in the case, and these are often many. Let me show you a common example.

Here is an ordinary case: A suit for damage caused by negligence. The questions that arise are few, compared to many other suits, but are enough to puzzle untrained minds.

Was plaintiff injured as he claims, and if so, where, how, and when, and how much was he injured?

Was the defendant negligent as charged, and was this negligence the cause in whole or part?

Was plaintiff free from negligence contributing to cause his hurt, and when will he recover?

What has the plaintiff lost in earnings and expense, and what must he expend for further treatment?

What pain has he endured or must endure, and what sum of money will suffice to compensate him for his injuries?

These questions may seem simple, yet they are but names of groups of other questions, mixed together into one compound question, requiring expert skill to analyze, and thus divided into several parts, each part is still sufficiently complex to give an expert quite a task. The juror who can perform this feat must have a mental structure capable of thinking long and clearl. He must be able to sustain a train of thought in logical connection until each question in proper order and in just relation has met with its solution and each solution carried to the end has with the whole allied formed the criterion for his verdict.

These various questions are like many burdens laid on the steps that lead into a temple: the weak may take up one and carry it, but he who properly ascends must take and carry all until the top is reached, for all compose the basis of the verdict. This work requires a thinker of uncommon skill who has a mind that knows no master but the truth: a mere automaton or pipe through which another blows or plays upon is not sufficient.

All creatures have some reason and show ability to think about familiar things. Men of small minds may in their narrow sphere teach wisdom to the wisest, while men accounted great in intellect when forced outside the sphere of their experience will often fall and be the easy marks for fraud and crime.

Most men dislike to think out of their spheres. They save themselves the effort and adopt the notions of their fellows, or they follow blindly time-worn precepts of the honored dead. Great numbers seek a master who will assume to guide them and plan in their behalf. So when some low-browed egotist assumes superior knowledge, they adore him much, cling to and follow, and for his boldness give him wealth and most obsequious service. Let me present a type of these who always seek to be controlled.

Job Devotee.

He was a thin and rabbit-headed man, a blue nose blonde, with fine soft hair, long neck and bright blue eyes, and had a beg-your-pardon air about him. From youth he had been docile and obedient, followed the guidance of his parents, obeyed his teachers and employers and all who gave him orders without a question or misgiving. In politics he bore the torch, at church he passed the hat, in business was a body servant who wore his master's livery with pride.

He held the cup when others drank and waited at the door while others watched the play. He was a fashion plate in dress, in manners was a model, moved like a dancing master, and like a water spaniel fawned on the hand that fed him.

He quickly saw the thoughts and wants of other men, endorsed their notions and gratified their wishes. In the opera of life he was a shining member of the chorus, coming on call and standing where directed. He looked to others as his natural masters, and those the most presumptions thought exalted beings whom he was made to serve. Like to the vine that twines around the tree or moss that hugs the rock his plastic mind leaned clingingly on those who would direct him.

Sometimes this man was summoned on a jury and here in harmony with his whole life he echoed but the views of fellow jurors and signed the verdict which the others formed, having no more to do with guiding the course of justice than stokers at the steamer's furnace in steering it through stormy seas.

Many Job Devotees appear on juries, all juries have them, and thus the verdict rarely reflects the judgment of twelve men. Pretending to be such, it is a sham and well it may be asked, if filching money from a suitor by such contrivance is not as shameful as picking pockets, while pie tending to teach the loser moral precepts.

We claim a great regard for mental training and mark those of greatest skill. We tax ourselves to fill the land with schools and strive to train our youths in ways of wisdom. Our doctors, lawyers, ministers and merchants, mechanics, bankers, and tradesmen of every class all in one voice demand the aid of skill. In every public office in the land, we call for training with but one exception, and that is the jury. Our urchins when they play football with nothing but their pride at stake will not invite a team member ignorant of the game. And even wild geese flying over our heads move in good order, choosing as their leader one who knows the way that they would fly.

We love our courts and speak of them in terms of praise. Our constitution we believe a shield which none can pierce to take away our rights. We pass, amend and supplement our laws, striving to make each line the voice of justice. But what are constitutions, courts or laws, when those who sit in judgment know them not and have no skill to fit them to the facts, who pass on suits impulsively as careless children handle guns, having no skill to aim, but shoot at random, hitting anyone who happens in the way.

CHAPTER IX.

Firmness.

The verdict must be found by all the jurors. Each must endorse it as his own true judgment. This he should do in honest faith, because he so believes from all the facts. If he instead gives up his judgment to his fellow jurors, if weary of the long dispute and bitter wrangling he at last consents to sign a compromise not squaring with his personal judgment he thus deserts his post. He brings this fake into court and, by a falsehood uttered for the purpose, has it recorded as a legal verdict.

A juror should have moral fibre that doesn't distort not under opposition, but calmly hears and weighs with patience and holds his ground until new reasons convince him he should change. If this he has not, he is not a juror such as the law intends, but merely a clay dummy, which other hands may mould as they desire. Yet he is counted to make the panel, supposed to have twelve men.

The courts might not endorse this fraud, should it be shown, but like a secret poison mixed with food, the spurious dose appears a legal verdict, and so it is swallowed and does its vicious work without detection. Most men do not possess this moral fibre. They yield to win the goodwill of the crowd.

How many vote for unfit men to please their friends? How many break their sacred ties and put aside the claims of conscience to gain the title of good-fellowship? Few can be trusted to handle wealth of others or their own, because they lack the courage to refuse the many who would borrow. Heads sound and sane in many ways are often soft in this. They drop the jewels that are genuine and choke the righteous throbs of conscience that they may chase the butterflies of present favor, and gather glittering gewgaws. Let me present one of the best of these:

Jeremiah Jellyfish.

He was in youth instructed in the best of schools and made familiar with all moral precepts. He was a model son of model parents, taught in the lore of all the ages, and filled with all the facts of modern science. His were the graces that adorn the cultured, the arts and manners of gentility that pass as current coin at every counter. Nature had blessed him with much manly beauty. In form and face he was a model fit for a statue of a Grecian god. A noble brow adorned with chestnut curls, a beard that Mars might envy, eyes bright with quick intelligence, yet beaming tender sympathy, a skin as white as milk save where the hue of health flushed his full lips. Tall and erect he stood among his fellowmen and looked like one made by the hand of Nature to command and lead mankind from darkness into light.

His fine proportions were not made to mask a mental weakling. His mind was broad and comprehensive as his noble brow. Memory held her place and did most perfect work. Reason was ever active and quickly grasped effects and causes in their proper sequence. And far above the whole a well-instructed conscience sat and watched the compass pointing to the right.

His heart was warm for others' woes, his hand outstretched to render aid. Firmly he held himself upon the narrow path of personal purity, yet looked with charity and love on all who took the broad and downward road to vice and crime. So general was his kindly sympathy that all accounted it a privilege to have his company. He spoke the right word in the proper place and did the fit thing when the time arrived. He mingled with the grave and gay and was enjoyed by all.

No liquor ever touched his lips, and yet among the drinking and the drunk he found warm welcome. His character for morals wore no stain and yet the vicious often invited him and at their orgies found his presence no reproof.

A church of orthodox belief held him a member of a high repute. Meanwhile he counted as his dearest friends agnostics of the strongest kind. In politics he bore a public part, aiding with voice and pen the party of his choice, but kept his words so free from bitterness that none opposed by him felt enmity. Employers and employed often waged a bitter war. Each asked his aid. He spoke as he believed, and those he spoke against loved him no less, so soft and gentle were his words and moderate were his views. In all things was he blessed. Health, wealth, domestic peace, were his in fullness. His neighbors, city, state and country held him in high esteem and took delight to do him honor. Fortune turned ever toward him her sweetest smile and showered on him her richest bounties. Such are the blessings sometimes won by easy grace and prudent conduct when skillfully employed by one endowed by Nature with a shining front.

This rare and radiant man was sometimes summoned on a jury. How did his heavenly plumage fit the jury box? He understood the evidence, and court's instructions, and all the points brought out in argument he easily discerned, his memory carried well the load until the jury room was reached, and there he listened patiently to what all his fellow jurors had to say and modestly expressed his own opin-

ion. He had no bias or wish to favor either side, and formed a judgment on the facts presented, in strict accordance with the law, as given by the court. And such had been his verdict, but his fellow jurors were moved by other motives.

Inflamed to fever by the closing speech they had forgotten many facts and many others misremembered, and disregarding all the court's instruction, they were in haste to find a verdict, written by their indignation. This wise man sought to stay their haste and call them to the bar of reason, but found the effort vain.

Their minds were set against the ground he took. He then tried several times to compromise and bring the others to him. He found them quite unyielding, but finally they moved a little way and he then went the rest and drank the bitter draught that they had mixed for him. Then with them he went before the court and solemnly declared this base child of their bias was an offspring of his judgment.

This way the law's intention was set aside because this man of noble parts was lacking in the moral strength to stand by his own judgment. There frequently are jellyfish found on the jury, but rarely have they such a mental grasp. In many walks of life they fill their places well and in the march of human progress give great aid, but on the jury they become poor timber, likely to warp or break when strength is most required They find countless reasons for that. Some-

times they urge expenses of another trial would put the party plundered in a worse condition, sometimes predict another jury would go further still in the wrong; they often put the blame upon the losing lawyer for not excusing certain jurors.

When conscious guilt needs badly an excuse, none is too thin for service as its cloak. The jurors who desert the post of duty for bribes or fear or lack of moral strength, show often in their faces, when they hear the verdict read the signs of their debasement. They hang their heads in shame or carry them too proudly, and when they answer to the usual questions asked they either speak too low, in sneaking accents, or else in tones of loud defiance, covering their guilty tracks with hummocks, that easily are seen.

CHAPTER X.

Talesmen.

Jurors drawn to make the panel are summoned to the court and there attend for several weeks to try such cases as require a jury. Those are the regular panel. When for any cause more jurors are required, the sheriff summons persons sitting in the court to act as jurors, or goes out and summons men he finds at work or on the street. These are denominated "talesmen."

The power to pick these talesmen for the cause is quite important to the sheriff. Sometimes he uses it to help his friends who seek employment on the jury, sometimes to get the kind of jurymen a certain party may desire. The sheriff rarely does the work himself. His deputy, known as a bailiff, performs the task. This practice has produced a type of juror called "professional," and thereby some succeed in getting many years of jury service.

There is a city in my native state to which my mind with loving memory turns. It sits in majesty on gentle hills where two bright, softly flowing rivers blend. Its people hold the highest rank for moral worth and high ideals, and her many courts for probity and lore are famed. Its bar maintains the loftiest seat for learning and professional skill, and rarely has corruption reached its court or juries with its slimy hand. Here the writer practiced law for many years. Here talesmen often occupied the jurybox.

A man who once resided there was absent from the city for many years. On his return great changes had occurred. He saw paved streets where formerly were swamps, and mansions of rare beauty sat upon the hills that had been barren when he went away. Large business blocks displaced the shacks that stood along the thoroughfares. A splendid courthouse took the place of shabby ruins on the public square, and on that hill where once a shattered statehouse stood, he found a gorgeous capitol raising on high its golden dome. Wherever he went he noted many changes and did not feel at home, until he came into the court and there found the selfsame men upon the jury, as on the day he left.

Looking down the vista of the years I still recall some faces that I saw before me on the jury when I practiced there. I seldom missed them from the court. They were of that peculiar type that much abounds where talesmen are in use. This I will try to sketch by putting forward my old friend

Waverly Weathercock.

He was a modest, unassuming man, with nothing very good or bad about him. His parents had been well to do, but with advancing years their means decreased and then he came to want. He had been educated well, but when he tried to get a place to earn his livelihood he found it very difficult because he had not learned a trade and had no skill for any special work. The gentle tasks that he could get to do lasted not long nor did they bring much pay. He had a constant strain to keep himself afloat in that swift moving social sea where he was supposed to swim.

He met and loved a girl whose parents also had been well to do. She had good taste and many wants, but she had learned to fit them to her purse, and when these two were wed, they made a shift to live the best they could. She rented rooms, served meals and did such fancy work as she could find employment for, and in many ways assisted to sustain the home.

He worked about the house, helped her to wash and clean, and cook and mend, relied on her to think and plan and

acted as her general errand boy. They manage to exist and make a good appearance on the meager sum which jointly they acquired, but nothing could they save for feeble age. They read the public library books, the latest magazines upon its shelves, and took a daily paper, and in that way kept in touch with the doings of the world.

They made associates of the cultured class talked much of poetry and art, and held a place as critics in the literary world. They found no fault with their pinched lot and always seemed content, and made a mimic show that well concealed the pressing needs that vexed them constantly. The years went, and he had passed his prime, and was no longer fitted for the little tasks which once he did, and had no fitness then for greater ones.

He drew no pension from the government, nor had he claim on any public fund, except perhaps a refuge at the poorhouse the county kept for all its indigent. Anyway, even this claim he did not care to make, so as a last resort to drive away the wolves of want, he hung about the court, and sought a place as talesman on the jury. The sheriff was his friend and wished to favor him in every way he could, so when talesmen were needed to fill up the box, this needy gentleman was chosen.

He always testified that he was qualified. He never had an interest in the ease, nor had he heard of it before. He was without the slightest bias on the subject matter and had no *wish to aid or injure either party, and so he seemed an ideal juror, and rarely was he challenged or removed. He listened patiently to all proceedings and understood them better than the average juror, and kept his mind in equipoise until the evidence was in, and when the jury were in consultation to settle on the verdict they should find, he seldom spoke or ventured an opinion, but voted without a word the secret ballot.*

He kept with the majority and signed the verdict that they wished. He had no force to stand by his opinion. His poverty made him as yielding here as he had ever been through life. He did not dare to hang the jury or refuse to take the way the largest number went, lest he might lose his chance to sit again. Thus, he was little worth and scarcely earned the little money paid for his weak service.

When the verdict was announced he sought the party who had lost the case and told him he had done his best to get a verdict in his favor, but all the other jurors were opposed. This also did he tell the losing lawyer and so fished for a favor where he could, paving the way for further jury service. In this way for many years he kept away from the almshouse by the sums he earned from sitting on the jury.

In justice courts the jurors all are talesmen brought by the constable out of the street, or taken from loungers in the court. In some states the laws require that they be paid by the side that asks a jury. The sum required for this is deposited in court before jurors are required to sit. When this is done, the officer often makes sure jurors know, whose money pays the fees, and justice jurors in large cities are often of such timber that any constable can bend them to his purpose.

The party paying for the jury rarely fails to get the verdict they want, if one is found. In other states the jury fees in justice courts are taxed as costs, and when the costs are paid the fees are given to the jurors. If not, the jurors get no fees. Where laws like these prevail, the jury often finds out which party can be made to pay the fees, then beat him in the suit to get their pay.

The writer knew a case in such a court, where quite unmindful of their fees a jury found their verdict against the party who had no means. When they brought their verdict into court, the venal justice chidingly exclaimed, "See what you've done. How can we ever get our fees?".

This is how all forms of legal justice is so cheaply bought and sold. There definitely are exceptions, and sometimes honest juries are obtained of talesmen, even in justice courts, and jurors sometimes put aside their own advantage and stoutly stand for right and duty. But the hope that they will keep this path is so uncertain, that few have faith in such a verdict as representing law or justice. Jurors are rarely summoned in large cities to sit in justice courts, unless the party knows the case is bad and thinks it worth the cost of paying for a jury to make the other side appeal.

Jurors should be composed of men whose capital transcends the little sum that comes from jury service so clearly that such considerations can cause no bias in their minds. The law that bribes the empty handed jurors to find a verdict of a certain kind that they may get their pay, reaches the highest point of folly, and is in keeping with all the other features of this stupid system.

CHAPTER XI.

Aggregated.

Herein have I considered many jurors, set down some faults that brand them as unfit, and tried to show the weakness of the many links which form the chain. Now let us test the chain itself and see if it is stronger than these several links. Some may contend that taken as a whole the jury has the strength of all its parts and that the verdict which they jointly find will represent the added strength of each. May be all the character, skill, intelligence and wide-experience possessed by each will be combined into a compound equal to the sum of all the several parts. This notion may look fair, but being searched with close analysis will prove unsound.

Graces of mind don't add. Each soul stands by itself, its virtues can not be transferred by simple mathematics. 'Tis said some statisticians wished to cross a stream and finding out its depth at either side and in its middle from one who knew it well, they ascertained the average was below their stature and thus concluded they could ford the stream. They attempted it and they were drowned. Their figures were correct but not in application to the stream. It had no average depth but was to them as deep as in its deepest part.

No quantity of fraud makes an honest man, no sum of fools make a sage. It is believed that in counsel there is safety. The truth of this depends upon the qualities of those who consult. If they are rogues who plot for fraud or crime there is no safety for their victims. If they are imbeciles, the combination of all their follies will have no attributes of wisdom. 'Tis true the jury may consult together and each impart some knowledge to the others, and thus the sum of all will make something greater.

Here all addition ceases, for in the end each juror should base the verdict on his own judgment. This verdict, therefore, cannot rise, when all tides are in flow, above the stature of the highest juror. This is the loftiest mark that ever is attained and never is this reached on any controverted question unless the

weaker minds and wills of the others are made sub-servient to the best man on the jury. Most verdicts fall below.

The wise and fair, in small proportion to the other jurors, must yield to ignorance and brutal bias or else no verdict is secured. This sometimes is a mere surrender, delivering arms and baggage to the opposition and making no conditions, but usually it is a treaty which compromises for a part of that which conscience claimed as due.

The plaintiff, not entitled to recover, receives the major portion of his spurious claim. The one whose cause is just, receives only a fraction of his due. This counterfeit of justice comes as the final product of a bitter wrangle, where many speak at once and more than once, using strong epithets and vulgar threats, charging corruption, bias, and the worst of motives.

Fractions are formed among the jurors, led by the hottest-headed on each side. These shout and swear and threaten and berate, and with a view of final compromise each fraction makes the most preposterous claims. This conflict is protracted until a stage of weariness is reached where memory is almost blank. Then by ignoring law and evidence and all opinions they have formed therefrom, the jurors sign a compromise which all agree to call a verdict. In the end brute force becomes the winner as in the days when suitors tried their suits by battle. Each champion beat the other with a stave of wood and he who first succumbed was then adjudged as in the wrong.

In jury trials, as they are conducted, the suitors now appear by substitutes. No longer staves of wood decide the contest, but words quite as offensive strike the ears, break down the stubborn wills and make the weaker yield. This way one bold juror, made noisy by the bribe that hired him to decide the question wrong, may force the honest members of the jury to come to his position or prevent a verdict, and defeat the object of the trial. Most bribes are given by defendants, who putting forward sham defenses are pleased to block the wheels of justice and defeat an honest claim by delay at least. Thus in the strength to find an honest verdict the aggregated lengths of this judicial chain are no whit stronger than its weakest link.

The author never sat upon a jury and hence his facts are hearsay, when applied to tell the secret workings of this body. The emanations from a secret chamber may give sure hints of what takes place within. Foul odors don't fly from flower beds where only roses bud and bloom. Vile epithets with coarse and boisterous clamors rarely salute the ears from happy homes. The exhalations from a jury room so far as one can hear

who stands outside are not assuring of deliberation, and cause less hope for justice than distrust.

For many years the author has attempted to ascertain from jurors when discharged the leading reasons for their verdict, both in his cases won and eases lost. He thus has had more than a hundred answers, and of the many can not now recall a single one that stayed to reason, or did not violate the court's instructions. Here are a few that well may serve as samples for the others.

In a suit brought by a widow for her husband's death, caused by a street car striking him, she was defeated. The reason given was that she had collected much insurance which she had placed upon his life and therefore had sustained no loss.

Another case brought for an injury to the head resulting in paresis: the claimant met defeat and this is the reason as stated by a juror: another person whom the juror knew once had a harder blow upon the head and did not have paresis.

In many suits brought by depositors of a bankrupt bank against defendants who had once been partners in the bank and had retired, the question was whether the plaintiffs knew these partners had left the bank when making their deposits, or had they actual notice that the change was made? The plaintiffs had executed many checks bearing the new firm name, deposited on blanks with its recital, and had deposits entered in a book containing it in large black letters, yet in nine cases out of ten defendants were defeated and the reasons given were in most cases these: Some said they thought defendants had a bond to keep them free from loss ; and others, that they should have taken one when they retired. A few spoke of the plaintiffs' poverty and of defendants' riches, and the sum defendants made in selling out.

A lawyer claimed $2,000.00 for a fee. The issue was the amount. I saw a statement of the ballots taken. One juror fixed the sum at $50 and one $2,000; some said $500. Some put the sum at less and others more, and after nineteen ballots had been taken nine hundred dollars was the sum agreed. The one who voted fifty dollars gave me the facts and said he still believed the sum he fixed sufficient, yet signed the verdict to save expenses of another trial.

Often the jury add the sums suggested by the several jurors and then divide the amount by twelve and take the quotient as their verdict. Thus do they mix their several judgments in a kettle and stirring it, dip out a one-twelfth part and call it justice.

If every juror gave a written reason for that strange compound which is called a verdict, and wrote that reason without aid, the general public would be so disgusted that they would rise against the jury system.

But all sit silent while the case is tried. Many have high-browed heads and look quite wise, and what is done when making up their verdict is veiled in mists of secrecy, and, thus disguised, their ignorance is hid, and when at last they come before the court and solemnly declare a certain verdict to be their well-considered, combined judgment the public by their fair appearance are hoodwinked and induced to trust the jury system. If they could only see behind the veil that hides the ugly features of this false prophet who claims to have transcendent beauty, the cheat would be discovered and his duped admirers would put him out of business.

The thought that fortunes, liberty and life are held by such a tenure that all may lose them at the whim of such as may compose a jury should stir us into action and demand a system more in accord with reason.

CHAPTER XII.

Effects.

The here have much effect upon the suitors, lawyers and the public. The preacher writes his sermons for his flock, a journal's readers guide the writer's pen, buyers select the merchant's stock. In this way the jury shapes the lawyer's course.

He crooks his knees and twists to win their favor, he strives to take advantage of their faults that he may win a verdict for his client. If he appeals to motives that are base, he deems the jury governed by such motives, thus the bar indirectly debased. All methods urged for better ethics at the bar will fall far short, while juries are composed of men whose minds are swayed by vicious pleas. Judges may preach and writers write and both may paint upon the heavens the lustrous image of eternal truth and beg all lawyers to bow down before it.

Some lawyers still will falsify the facts, make pleas of lying fabrics and bring forth to touch the juror's sympathetic nerves, a mass of matter not in evidence. Suitors anxious for success will seek such lawyers for their 'advocates and let the truthful starve.

The fickle public praising him who wins will wink and smile approvingly. Untill the jury box is purged of minds untrained and subject to such pleas, will there be no hope to purify the bar. [1]

Now take the loss the suitors suffer because of frailty in the jury box. A jury trial is a game of chance where he who wins must often lose by winning. Verdicts obtained are set aside because against the evidence, and thus the case is often tried again, until the substance of the final judgment is wasted in the costs of many trials. The case often goes to a higher court and, there

---

[1] "So? Anne!"
Anne was on the springboard; she turned her head. Jubal called out, "That house on the hilltop-can you see what color they've painted it?"
Anne looked, then answered, "It's white on this side."
Jubal went on to Jill, "You see? It doesn't occur to Anne to infer that the other side is white, too. All the King's horses couldn't force her to commit herself... unless she went there and looked and even then she wouldn't assume that it stayed white after she left."
"Anne is a Fair Witness?"
"Graduate, unlimited license, admitted to testify before the High Court
R. Heinlein, Stranger in the Strange Land

reversed, comes back, is tried again before another jury, again appealed, reversed and tried again, and thus the shuttle goes from court to court and then returns and makes another trip, weaving a shroud of loss for every party to the suit.

Ten years are often spent before a suit reaches a final judgment, when two had been sufficient if the jury who tried it first had all been fit. And when the final verdict has been rendered, it rarely has a just appearance, the product is a compromise which gives the suitor but a part of what he justly claims as due, or gives him judgment for a claim that's false. The courts grow weary of the many trials, despair of justice, and in the end allow the verdict most unjust of all to stand.

The suitor for the honest claim then counts the sum of trouble he has had, the years of anxious care and large expense, and chides himself that he did not consent to being robbed without the jury's aid. Nor is this all: the suitor winning on a spurious claim gives hope to many knaves of similar success and suits are brought by thousands who possess no rights, because of hope that a jury will go wrong

On the other hand, a multitude of honest claims are never sued, claimants preferring to lose the whole, rather than go to great expense and lose the greater part. Such are the loss, expense, distrust and disap-

pointments brought to suitors in civil suits by jury faults. But these are small when matched against the loss that follows prosecutions for crime.

If the case is one of general notoriety, the getting of a jury is a task prodigious, weeks and often months drag on in weary pace, while judge and lawyers strive to get a jury in the box. Thousands are summoned from their tasks of toil, brought to the court and they're examined and if perchance some rumor flying on uncertain wing has reached their ears and lodged, 'tis feared their simple, untrained minds have thus been biased and hence they are excused and thousands more are summoned. This slow process wastes the public funds, depletes the means of those accused and causes losses to the many men thus summoned to the court.

When the jury is procured by all this mighty labor, it is so weak and frail it may convict the innocent on mere suspicion or be cajoled by advocates to let the guilty go. The public pays enormous bills for costs made necessary by such trials, when all the points in issue could be better tried with slight expense, if done without a jury, or the law had planned a jury of men well trained for jury service. The public and the private loss might be endured without complaint and all its victims well might smile if by the sacrifice the precious boon of justice were procured.

Such, alas, is not the case — the jurors chosen are so unfit to do the work intrusted in their hands that all the burdens laid on them, on suitors and the public are worse than wasted because their verdicts are but cloaks which hide oppression in the guise of justice. So court expenses have become prodigious and yet grow greater every passing year, and like a cancer at the nation's vitals, gnaw deep and wide, threatening a speedy ruin.

Murder keeps up its carnival of bloody riots. Thieves of all kinds now ply their wicked trades and every kind of crime thrives go unmolested, while courts groan on their slowly moving wheels, years behind the criminal procession. The tools of burglars have been much improved and implements of crime reached high perfection, and yet the mode of trying criminal cases has made no progress since the Pilgrims landed.

The system first devised to fit the wants of feudal England, when laws were few and population scarce and men's chief fear the encroachments of the Crown. We still have with us as it stood when much of Britain was a wilderness.

Genius has filled the world since then with countless gifts to bless mankind, and yet we blush to admit that in our courts we still retain and practice unimproved worn-out antiquated modes of trial which once were useful to a barbarous people, but long ago must be gone for us and now are a serious hindrance to our progress.

CHAPTER XIII.

General Faults.

Selection.

The general method of selection is the blind-fold drawing. The law provides some officer to make a list. This list contains the names of voters, made up from those who voted at the last election. These are selected by the officer to suit his wishes, excluding those by law disqualified, and those who have a legal right to claim exemption. The names so taken are put on separate slips, placed in a box and then another officer, with bandaged eyes, draws from this box the names enough to make up a panel.

Those drawn are summoned to the court, sworn and examined. If they prove residents of the county, are qualified as voters, can read and write and have the sense of sight and hearing and are below a certain age they are accepted on the panel. Lawyers and doctors, clergymen and druggists, teachers and editors, and many public officers have legal right to be excused. Men whose engagements are important are usually let go and only those remain who can plead no excuse in law.

When any case is called for trial, the names thus on the panel are put on other slip's and mixed together, and the clerk draws from these haphazard until the jury box is filled. This is the usual method of selection. It varies somewhat in the different states but is essentially the same in every court, where jurors are employed. The object is to get a jury drawn from the body of the county who are its citizens. When in the box the jury are examined by the lawyers who represent each party to ascertain if they have any bias. If found related to either party or interested in the cause on trial, or they have formed opinions that are unqualified, about the merits of the suit, they may be challenged as unfit. Most states provide for challenges by either party, for which no reason need be given. These are called "peremptory" and the number fixed by law according to the nature of the case. The place of every juryman excused is by another filled until the jurors on the panel have all been called, then talesmen may be summoned to fill the box. Such are the usual methods used to get a jury.

The part blind chance plays in the game is most important. On this alone all must rely. Once men were slaves of superstition. Then mighty rulers watched the flight of birds, or killed them and searched their entrails and by what they saw or found decided between war and peace. And sages far-famed for learning noted the incoherent words of those insane or drunk and deemed them oracles by which the gods revealed their wills to men.

Now it seems foolish, but is it any worse than letting chance decide the character of a jury? If chance should be the arbiter in courts then why not throw a die or flip a coin and thus decide the suit without a trial? The just decision of a case according to the law and fact requires an expert knowledge. Would anyone select a surgeon, a lawyer or a judge, by drawing blindfold from a box such names as chance might give from the legal voters? Would any sane man hire this way an agent for even common work? This method is so strikingly absurd that dwelling on it further seems a waste of time.

It may be said the reason why this grab-bag game is played is to secure a fair, impartial drawing, that we so much lack faith in public officers, that we rather trust to luck than to their judgment. This belief is quite as foolish as the system. There is no game of chance where cunning may not intervene to stack the cards or load the dice, or in some other way contrive to cheat those who rely on fickle fortune. But none is quite so easy as this one. It needs no expert skill to so arrange the names and draw the panel as to pack the jury. The officer who does the drawing is rarely closely watched. If he be plastic to designing bribers he has no trouble to get a jury suited to their desires. He who is so simple-minded that he will pin his faith for honest jurors on such a method of selection lacks knowledge of the ways of rascals.

The law should fix the qualities that fit for jury service. These should include education, skill and training and well-known character for honor as will be needed to discharge the task imposed. Qualified people might be selected by other men appointed by the courts of last resort as a commission for that purpose and thus a list made up from which to draw the panel.

When this list was made and furnished to the court, the judge might draw his panel, selecting from the list the best names he could find thereon, according to the knowledge which he has or information that he can obtain, striving at all times to procure those best adapted to the service, aud freest from suspicion. If jurors were selected, they would be fitted when first required to sit and by experience would improve. Then would the right arm of the court be worthy of its place and not be paralyzed as now by unfit men. The judges who had power to so select would have a pride in their selection, getting the best men they could find.

The method proposed here may not be perfect and doubtless many better may be found, but the present system is so bad that almost any change would better it, and surely one is sorely needed. This weak spot in our judicial fabric grows weaker every day.

In former years cases were few, amounts in question small, and few the efforts to corrupt the jury. Great changes are occurring in the sum and character of the causes. Vast fortunes now are passing through the courts and changing hands in lawsuits and much larger sums depend upon the verdicts. With this increase has come increased temptations and a strong demand for better men to fill the box. Meanwhile the growth of cities and the spread of crime has made the mass to draw from more uncertain. The blindfold method will no more suffice and must give place to one insuring fitness, or else our courts will soon become the playground of corruption where scheming agents of designing suitors will pack the jury with their minions, ready to sign the verdicts they have written.

The verdict must be found by all the jurors. All must agree. This feature is anomalous. The nation's highest court, composed of only nine, decide the fate of millions by a majority of one. This judgment of five men may shatter solemn acts which Congress has declared to be the law. The highest courts in all the states may thus declare their judgment. Congress and legislatures pass their bills and corporate boards manage the millions in their hands. If bills required the vote of all to pass, few laws would be enacted and the business of the nation could easily be blocked by fools or knaves.

If mere majorities may pass our laws and mere majorities construe their meaning and set aside the jury's verdict, then in the name of all consistency, why should the will of one be able to prevent a verdict by the other jurors? And yet, our legislators remain so blind that they bow down before this jury fetich, decayed and moss-grown with its hoary age, and dare not make the slightest change.

The writer for many years was in the crowd who worshiped without reason. Cases requiring many weeks for trial were tried once, twice and thrice, and every time one juror blocked a verdict until from waiting weary years the plaintiffs were exhausted and made a compromise, recovering but a fraction of that they claimed as due, and by the eleven on the jury considered just. Yet so sacred did he deem this idol that he could not consent to change its ugly form or take away one worm that burrowed in its moss. If seven of the twelve could find a verdict jurors would seldom disagree, and much loss occasioned by mistrials would be avoided. More compromises would occur and verdicts might approach to justice.

The Number.

Another feature is the number. Israel had twelve tribes, and Christ had twelve apostles, therefore must we have twelve men on the jury? These are the only reasons I can conjure up. If weight of flesh were useful the number would add power, or if the task could be divided into sections each juror might take a part and number be the means of speed. But neither fact exists. Since every juror must do all the work, must hear all evidence, remember all, and all consider, and form a judgment on his own account, the number is a brake and not a help. As well it might be fifty or a hundred as just a dozen.

The nation's highest court, as I have shown, contains but nine; most state courts of the highest sort but six or seven, and some have only three. From their high perches these great courts decide the weightiest matters and give decisions that are final. Why then should twelve men be required to try a simple case, thus subject to review by courts of one or three or seven. The number some may say secures deliberation which would not be the case if one man was the jury. This I concede has force.

Each controverted question has two sides and two may represent these sides, and lest they might stand one and one against each other and so no verdict be obtained, a third might well be added; thus two of three could find a verdict. I find no basis for a larger number and think that three, except in matters of the highest import might well suffice to form a jury. These should be qualified and then their judgment would be as likely to be right as are the courts of last resort which hear the case from printed abstracts.

CHAPTER XIV.

Restricted Juries.

A most important branch of jurisprudence now has no jury. In chancery cases, which involve great questions of both law and fact and large sums are at stake, no jury is allowed unless the chancellor thinks that he needs a jury to advise his conscience. This seldom is required, and when he gets a verdict he may disregard it. The judge who sits to try these chancery suits, sits also on the law side of the court, where every suitor may demand a jury on every controverted question, and must have one unless he waives it.

Thus the same man, whom we trust to try disputes involving millions, if the suit is brought on one side of the court, may not determine the most trifling issue if on the other side without the verdict of twelve men. And these two sides are merely legal fictions.

Once they had meaning. The system that we call the common law grew like a tree. Its trunk was rooted in the throne of England, and sent out a branch providing many forms of action, in which the king was forced to grant a jury. Finding these forms of action incomplete, judges grafted to the trunk of this great tree another branch providing for another form of suit which they assumed to try without a jury, claiming its nature needed greater wisdom than the jurors would possess. This tree we have transplanted with these branches and here it grows, both branches drawing forces from the self-same roots, and having fruit of like variety, are practically the same, but still we keep the fiction that was framed on foreign soil.

The same judge sitting on one branch declares himself a court of common law, when on the other branch a court of chancery. Now bring to view the whole and we can plainly see how foolish the distinction. If we can trust a single judge to try one suit, why not another, with no greater sum at issue? And why may not the jury be abolished in common law as well as chancery suits? Most lawyers have a leaning toward the jury, so has the writer, and would retain some form of it in every case where any reason can be found, but we must search in vain to find a reason for its use in civil suits.

Where claims are small one judge learned in the law and trained at hearing evidence ought to suffice, and where the sum involved does not exceed live hundred dollars, to bring in other men to aid who have less skill and training seems a waste of time, especially when his judjment is reviewed by other judges on appeal.

Where the sum in question exceeds this sum and the greater risk might call for other men to share it, two might be added, and two of this three determine the decision. The judge or judges who decide the case should find the facts, and all the evidence offered by either party should be admitted, except where all who sit find it irrelevant. This evidence and facts so found should constitute the record on appeal and there the case should be decided on its merits, and final judgment entered.

In this way we would have a speedy trial and termination of the case, and escape the game of battle door and shuttlecock so often played by courts. This would rid us of a mass of questions which now so often cause us trouble relating to the proper functions of the court and jury. The law makes jurors judges of the facts in many cases, and courts are judges of the law.

Most cases are so mixed with questions of both law and fact that what is strictly law and what is strictly fact becomes most difficult, for at the last analysis all laws are facts and facts are often laws.

So where the judge's province has its end and where the jury's does begin breeds close distinctions, which depend upon the fineness of the sight of him who views them. The minds of learned courts so often disagree that myriads of cases are reversed and tried again because forsooth the upper court believed the lower court had erred in taking from the jury or in not taking some question as it ought. Great losses are incurred to suitors by this conflict, which usually is remote, and touches not the substance of the suit, and in the end does nothing but decide who should decide the case, not how decide it. The losses thus sustained are large indeed, but small when set against the enormous waste now caused by bad instructions to the jury, or those which upper courts may hold are bad.

About one-third of all the suits appealed return for second trial because of faults in this respect. The jury are supposed to know no law, which probably is true. They are supposed to get knowledge from the court which probably is not. The fine distinctions made in legal points mean nothing to the jury, and yet the courts must logically presume that they are understood, and that instructions faulty in the least degree may have worked serious harm, and so ten thousand errors have arisen and caused re- verses which really had no bearing on the verdict. The train of woes, defeats and disappointments springing directly from this source are quite beyond our calculation. Thus often have the claims possessing greatest merit suffered delay until the death or loss of witnesses have compassed their defeat; and others have been wasted in protracted trips from court to court. The abolition of the jury in civil suits would bring relief from losses such as these.

The claim is often made that damage suits necessitate a jury trial. Such damages can not be calculated by any certain standard. Pain, loss of health, beauty or reputation rely for compensation on opinions, and these may be as numerous as the persons who compose the jury. Hence, it is said, twelve average men can give a better estimate than any judge. If that be true, why should the judge have power to nullify that estimate and set aside the jury's verdict?

My observations lead me to believe the supposition is not true. The average jury has no skill to justly pass on damage claims. They can not separate the loss from liability to pay the loss. Being on a sympathetic tide that carries all before it they but see the loss sustained and don't ask for the fault that caused it. The courts contrive in every way to check this sympathy and go to great extent in nullifying verdicts. If they did not and gave to the jury all the sway the law intends, the stream of wealth required to pay such claims would ruin every public corporation and many private parties.

An injury so slight that had it happened from an accident on which no suit was brought, it would have scarcely had a moment's thought, becomes of such importance when magnified in court by plaintiff and his witnesses that all the savings of a thrifty life would scarce suffice to pay the verdict.

To save themselves from verdicts such as these defendants go great lengths in devious ways. They hire most artful counsel to cajole the jury, to coax and flatter them and win attention from the plaintiff's wrongs to their sleek persons. They use the officers of the court to juggle with the panel, thus getting for their cases the hardest hearts and closest purses, whose itching palms may easiest be reached. They line the pockets of the judge with passes or other so-called courtesies designed to make him mellow. They sweeten relatives of the jurors with sly, ambiguous favors, expecting that the sugar-coated dose will somehow work upon the jury. When the sum involved will warrant such a risk, they send out under cover of the night agents with bribes to visit homes of jurors.

By these and many other underhanded ways, defendants in these damage claims have nullified to great extent the vast advantages which a jury otherwise would give the plaintiffs. Here then, as elsewhere, there are natural checks by which one wrong, in part, off-sets another. A jury eager to despoil the rich man's purse and help the claimant, whether right or wrong, begets defendants who for self-defense will use the vilest means to hang the jury, and judges who know the jury's bias are easily inclined as far one way as jurors are the other.

Because of these abuses by which both judge and jury are disabled from forming fair, unbiased judgments, the just claim has no better chance than it would have without a jury. Three well-trained, upright judges, scorning to favor either party, would be far safer for the honest claim than this bad mixture of biased judge and jury, and he whose claim was false would be quite certain of defeat. Men trained to judge are not less tender to human suffering than the common mass that are untrained, nor are they less inclined to value loss sustained by hurts and slander. And where the facts and law create a right of action, they are more prone to give fair compensation than men of less learning. But they place above their sympathies the duty that the law enjoins, and so allow no spectacle of woe to move them to forsake it.

It is therefore my belief that in this class of suits a jury is not needed. There is, however, one consideration which makes me hesitate. Due partly to the jury system, as I before have stated, and partly to a lust for power and gain, great combinations of the corporate type have grasped the government in all its branches. Their tentacles have touched the seat where sits the judge. Their lobbies whisper in his ears the welcome promises of future favor. They bring to bear upon the bench seductive arts, well planned to win weak men, and by their minions they so pull the wires of politics that weaklings find a pathway to the bench, and sometimes do they place thereon the men who many years have been their servants.

Such power they now possess with prospect of increase as years go by, that the procurement of three upright men to hold the balance fair in cases such as these might prove most difficult; and now therefore it' there is a reason, which I do not concede, that we should still retain the jury in these cases, it must be as the price of our abasement, because we can not trust ourselves to place upon the bench the competent and honest men who should be there.

The jury as we have it now is but a weak protection in any case and weaker grows from day to day, beomes a greater burden, clog, and means to cause delay with every passing year, until a trial has become a long-continued game of chance, bringing discredit on our courts and ruin to the righteous suitors. If jurors are retained, they should be made of better men to give us much protection, should be reduced in number and a mere majority empowered to find a verdict. The laws should guard with greatest care all steps in their selection. Men worthy of the highest trust should do the work, having a good chance of getting on the jury list the names of those most fit for jury service. If those whose waxing riches have placed them at the top in power would use their means to purify the bench and not debase it, there is no doubt a jury would be a useless thing in trying civil cases.

The claim is sometimes made that lawyers are too technical and therefore unsafe judges where the facts are close and evidence conflicting, and that it is far better to have the laity per- form this work. I see no force in this objection against the bar, but if there is, and men not trained in law should sit in judgment on the facts in issue, then I suggest they sit upon the bench in seats of honor like sovereigns, having equal power and rank with other judges.

The jury now are captives, who sit like dummies, subject to the call of him we call the judge. Their function is important and if they are worthy to discharge it they should be treated as we treat the judge. Let there be two of them instead of twelve and with one lawyer elected as the judge make up the court. This trinity could then decide all civil cases, each having privileges of taking notes and asking questions and using transcripts of the evidence in forming court opinions and equal voice in making up the judgment.

In prosecutions brought for crimes where life or liberty is at stake we have a different question. Money means much to its possessors and more to those who have it not, and yet most people hold it lightly, staking it upon the merest chance or casting it aside for whims and trifles. Life is the gift of heaven, and liberty its fairest, sweetest fruit, without which life seems but an empty cheat, and both are dear beyond compare, and should be treated as priceless boons in every court of justice.

No one should forfeit either until the proof is clear and leaves no room to doubt in the minds biased by suspicion, envy or revenge. If anyone the law has placed in judgment has doubt about the prisoner's guilt, when all the evidence has been heard and been considered, the verdict should acquit. And I go further still in favor of the accused.

If circumstances so surround the act and him who did the deed that mercy may be properly invoked, there is no place in all the land more fit to measure mercy and apply it than this, where all the facts are known, and in no office is it more becoming than at the judgment seat. After the question of a prisoner's guilt it should be asked: Is this a case to punish? And how much? And everyone who sits in judgment on the bench or in the jury box should vote for punishment as his own free judgment, before conviction is secured.

In ordinary accusations incurring but a fine or short jail sentence a trained and upright judge should be sufficient to decide the matter, and fix the punishment. subject to review upon appeal if one is taken. In accusations which may lead to terms in prison of one year or more, or to the taking of a life, three men should constitute the bench, save in a certain class of crimes where I would add a jury. Treason and government offenses and those which have their root in politics and may be punished by destroying life, should have a jury, when the accused requests it, who sit free from coercion by the bench, decide in secret, and must agree to cause conviction.

The object of this jury is to counteract the natural bias so likely to sway judicial officers in such a trial and give the victim a better chance to be protected from official power. The number that should form this jury is not an easy question. There is no basis on which to fix it. Twelve seems too many, six ought to be sufficient. This doubles the number sitting on the bench, and making nine in all. In order to convict, the nine should all agree beyond a doubt as to the prisoner's guilt, and that he has no claim to mercy. This judgment is subject to review upon its merits if defendant wishes to appeal, should give the culprit just protection and save him from the vengeance of his foes.

CHAPTER XV.

Choosing a Jury.

At common law the sheriff made a list and parties struck the names there from until a panel was secured. These were summoned and no challenges allowed except for cause. Most states have laws allowing challenges peremptory, where no cause is stated. Lawyers then may choose whom they will take and whom reject within the limits prescribed. Here is the riddle of the sphinx, that neither men nor stars have means to solve.

The fresh-fledged nestling from the schools with untried wing and high, ambitious hopes, may feel oppressed with knowledge which drizzles from his overflowing stock, and so have much to say on this. He merely strips his shoulders for the stripes which com-

ing years will bring. In many sad defeats he will un-
learn the lore so confidently held. The prudent veter-
an of a thousand battles, whose back is calloused with
the stings that disappointment gives, when asked for
his advice on this will shake his head and change the
subject. And I perhaps might better leave unsaid what
many readers wish to know.

On this dark point my fading torch is dim.
I claim no light beyond that common stock
Which years may bring to all who strive and suffer.

Long have I tried to read the minds of jurors;
Alas, the soul of man is like the face of Jove,
Veiled deep in clouds. [2]

Sometimes my nearest neighbor, chum, and confi-
dant has hung the jury and defeated me, and sometimes a man I knew an enemy, drawn in the box when
challenges were gone, has saved the verdict for me.

In fifty cases that I tried one year I had no adverse
verdicts. Another year in fifty-three I lost but two. And
in the following year suits which promised sure success met quick defeat and all my cherished hopes
crumbled like ashes in my hands.

---

[2] *(Editor's note)* I beg pardon from the reader for this unexpected wanna-be-
shakespeare piece of text. The original wording, however, was so beautiful-
ly rhythmed, that I could find no excuse to brush out that beauty and added
a couple words to make it a little longer instead.

Such is the sad uncertainty attending jury trials and show how far from perfect are all plans for picking jurors. Yet there are rules in guessing which have seemed to serve me well, and these I offer here for such consideration as they may deserve.

Juries should fit the case. Suits complicated with mixed questions requiring careful thought and nice distinctions need men of intellectual grasp. The lawyer who expects to win because his cause is just and tries to found it on the plaque of reason should strive for jurors who can understand the reasons that are urged. This is essential to the plaintiff and to defendant doubly so.

The latter must rely on mental strength to stand against the closing speech and so needs minds ranged on his side who can not be deceived by sophistry, or moved by strong appeals to passion. The suitor with a doubtful case but feebly bolstered in the evidence, depending more on pity than on law or facts, seeks more for hearts than brains.

Men of fat, ruddy faces, large eyes and portly bodies are suited to his plea and serve him better than high-browed and frowning men with deep-set eyes and forms of bony build, youths with bounding blood are better far for him than frosty age.

Some nations leave their impress on their subjects. This lasts for many years and often it appears upon a jury. The suitor of a foreign birth will often find a juror of a the similar origin much in his favor. Some nations have greater pity for the weak and some a stronger sense of duty.

These facts the lawyer should consider. Fathers feel more for children, husbands more for wives and widows than men who are not involved. A situation like the plaintiff's in age, vocation, wealth, or social status, has some effect to favor him and if the juror has sustained a wrong which bears a close resemblance to the one alleged, this makes him easy to convince.

Elements of prejudice like these appear in every jury and must be reckoned with. They rarely are decisive of the verdict, unless they move the leader of the panel. One man, more forceful than the rest, will often take the other jurors with him. This man is most important to discover before the jury is accepted, and if his composition does not fit your case he should be challenged and the leadership placed in the hands of one more fitted to your side.

On this point alone have more mistakes been made than any other. Most lawyers confident of power to argue and persuade prefer the mild-eyed, yielding juror to the stern and sober thinker with his hard, unsympathetic face, and on both sides a plastic jury is the object sought. The jury selected this way is mostly of this mettle and yet a few remain cast in a different mold, who have not been discovered or could not thus be challenged. One of these is sure to write the verdict.

In the world of men the wise select the leaders for alliance and they only count with common mass. They find the leader in the human flock and put their bell on him. This should the lawyer strive to do who picks the jury. In this, however, he must often fail.

While much is evident from outward signs, it often happens that the inner man does not display his excellence, and he who seems the weakest proves the strongest under test, and he who otters much assurance before the battle has begun proves but a weakling when the fight is on. Flamboyant airs often may deceive and make the shrewdest lawyer found his hopes on sand.

It is well to know the history of the man and if it fits his pompous seeming. Whether he be a trifler of the common sort or have that prowess that is wont to deal in weighty matters as if they were but trifles. When you have done all that the wisest man could do to get the best of juries sitting, the slightest thing may turn the whole awry and dash your hopes to dust[3]. Such is the frailty of a common jury.

To seek for justice at its hands is usually a vain pursuit. Attracted by its ancient source and democratic composition we think its lustre is the star that guides us to the sacred place where justice sits enthroned. We follow its alluring light with perfect trust and find at last it is the *ignus fatuus'* fatal gleam that leads us to the tangled swamp of wretchedness and ruin.

---

[3] *(Editor's note)*
When we have shuffled off this mortal coil,
Must give us pause.
With this regard their Currents turn awry.
And lose the name of Action.

Sorry, couldn't pass on it.

CHAPTER XVI.

Treatment of the Jury.

Considering these many frailties and all their side effects, how can a lawyer run his case that it shall suffer least and gain the most from it all? Each juror is a little tree with many tender branches and every branch is acutely sensitive in some respect and thus the twelve men on the jury become a wood, where he who moves about must take great care.

It is not safe to talk on general matters or wander from the point in issue or comment on an alien subject lest you may hit some juror in a tender spot and make him turn against you. A man who throws a stone into a crowd may wound a friend, and he who speaks against an institution or a general class, or by derision grills a witness for some defect in speech or manner may pinch a friendly juror and turn him to the other side.

Therefore, the advocate should never wander or strike a blow not surely aimed to hit a certain mark, nor should he show his personal likes or hates or make exposure of his views on any subject whole men may divide, lost thereby some one on the jury who holds a contrary view may much dislike the exhibition and look with disfavor or contempt upon the person making it. Nor should the lawyer put himself in evidence in any other way. The ease alone is what he has to try and certain questions only are submitted to the jury. What does not bear distinctly on these questions should be ignored, and all his strength and time be spent upon the issues. By this their untrained minds may be directed to the best advantage.

All men like praise and those enjoy it most who least deserve it. Juries are gullible to flattery and man lawyers use it with success. It is a dangerous weapon which each side may much employ and thus competing with each other go to excess and only win disgust from court and jury. The time taken by that from a true discussion and energy lost in it when added to the degradation caused thereby, make up a sum of loss which more than equals any gain there from.

The jury should be treated with great respect, becoming the high function they discharge. This tends to lift them to a lofty plane above the mists of petty bias, and here they should be kept free from unworthy motives.

He who believes his cause is just should be content with this and so will find a surer pathway to success. He who promotes a spurious plea, depending on confusion and vile motives for success, will always strive to drag the jury down from this high plane. He often may succeed, because their undeveloped minds do not detect false lights or closely note the lines where duty bids them move.

While such men are employed, the false will sometimes win and justice stumble or miscarry. Such sad results can be avoided, if at all, when he whose cause is just sticks to the higher plane and never in the least degree soils his clean hands with any kind of baseness.

The minds of untrained men are easily upset and turned awry by conflict and confusion; they move but slowly, and he is wise who hurries not or tries to hurry them. The advocate should take the necessary time to clearly make the point he undertakes, painting the background for the thing he would present, so that it will stand out distinct in all its parts, thus stamping on the juror's mind an image that will last until the consultation room is reached. 'Tis better far to make a few points clearly than many that are vague. Those feebly painted may be wiped away by what occurs thereafter and far before the jury reach the room.

Abstractions are unsafe. The tersest statements of the tritest truths will often fail when made to minds that act slowly and are dull in comprehension. Children use blocks to learn the forms of letters and pictures to acquaint themselves with words. Simple minds can be most easily made to understand by using clear forms and glowing images. Big pictures in strong lines will much impress, while lines of finer texture delicately traced, in soft, artistic tints, may have but slight effect.

The essence of the plaintiff's case lies in the wrong to be righted. This should the lawyer paint in colors glowing as the truth will warrant and give the strong-est setting that the facts will bear. All should be free and natural, not showing efforts to exaggerate. The consequences of this wrong and all its wide effects should have a full portrayal as they bear upon the state, the plaintiff and the law, that those who sit in judgment may freely comprehend what pleads for their remedy.

The burden of defendant's ease is innocence or an excuse. The facts that tend to show him faultless or lay the blame upon the plaintiff or some other person, or prove the injury an accident with none to blame, should all be mustered and set forth in strongest light that jurors having all in mind may fix the blame and measure the compensation. From first to last, all should be so contrived that it will give their untrained minds the fairest chance to comprehend the whole. This way the case will be fairly tried and justice done, if that be possible by such imperfect means.

CHAPTER XVII.

Bench, Bar, and Jury.

When I first turned to my pen in spring, I wanted to ease the burden that so long had laid upon my mind. My first theme was "Foibles of the Bench"[4]. From out the dusty chambers of the past I brought the visions of my early years and resurrected forms of long ago. From these I framed composites, hoping without offense to show thereby what chaos may be created by human weakness of the milder kind when lifted to that lofty seat. Some have received the message that I penned and sent to me their kindly words, and now I watch and wait to see the fruitage of the seed thus sown.

---

[4] *(Editor's note)* I have reworked this book as well, and you will find it in Legal Stories 1.0 series as «16 Pictures of the Bench»

When summer's reign was in its fullest prime I took again the pen and wrote of "Foibles of the Bar"[5] and launched the little craft upon the tide, hoping it might drift to sympathetic hands, where it would bless my brothers at the bar and those who might thereafter seek its foid. Nor was I disappointed here. It touched a tender chord which brought me sweetest music. A mother loves the babe she brought to life and feels a throb of heaven to hear it praised. So did the words come back to me that spoke of merit in my book.

Now in November's melancholy days, when chilling gusts sport with withered leaves, I stand again upon the rippling beach prepared to start another craft. Much do I fear it will not find the favoring gales that met my other ventures. Securely in its box the jury sits wreathed by the halo of the centuries, and well may smile at any words of mine however well directed. The multitude of broken hearts, the victims of its lack of skill, now beat no more. The long procession of the innocent, torn from their homes and carted to the scaffold, may not arise to plead again their causes.

---

[5] As you may guess, this book is also available on Amazon as «14 Pictures of the Bar» in Legal Stories 1.0 Series. They are all witty and the first two are, frankly speaking, easier to read and more lighthearted. So, if you somehow started with this one, I give you my apologies for the wrong start and invite you for another try with books about the Bench and the Bar.

Like unskilled surgeons are awkward with the knife, the juries' worst mistakes are in the tomb. Our earth has seen a deal of cruelty. The race in struggling upward toward the light has strewn its path with wrecks. Each institution that we cherish most began in wrong, and like the Hindoo Juggernaut crushed many prostrate victims while it onward moved, until at last by law of precedent, what once was wrong became a sacred right.

A straggling few of all the countless crimes appear on history's page. The most are lost to human annals. But of these few some of the blackest sort were fashioned by the courts. In these proceedings' juries had a hand. A tyrant rarely had a task so mean, so foul and full of blood and horror that he could not find a solemn-visaged, servile, oath-bound jury to give it righteous color by a verdict. But jurors have not acted on their own account, they have been truckling tools of stronger men; sometimes the dupes of despots, other times of mobs and always by the agency of lawyers.

Bench, bar, and jury box have often stood a trinity in crime and then the other two have made a scapegoat of the box, saddling their vilest sins upon the simple weaklings who have filled it. This is the rule in all affairs of life, the strong receive the profits and the weak get the blame. Yet after centuries the jury still retains its place within our courts, is still responsive to coercive means and swayed by bias and unworthy motives.

'Tis still a clog and impediment on the wheels of justice, the hope of knaves and cloak to cover crime. On every hand we see its errors, the numerous wrecks its blunderings have made in wasted fortunes and in ruined lives, and yet we venerate it for its age and clutch it as a rock of refuge.

When I survey the ground over which I've passed, writing of bench and bar, the jury and the court, the mass of faults that do appear to mar and block the courts in their high function and the enormous loss incurred thereby, I sicken at the sight. I can not hope these lines of mine will move these mountains in the path of progress, or even cut a trail across them.

The first explorer rarely scales the loftiest peaks. A few steps upward in the steep and flinty rock he cuts with patient toil and dies. Another starting where he ceased may cut a few steps more and be succeeded by another still, who also cuts and climbs until some future climber completes the task and stands upon the top and sees the glorious vision of the world beyond.

So I behold the labor here essayed, and hope these several efforts of my pen may prove so many steps that upward lead to truth in this regard and that when I, exhausted with my worn-out tools, must cease, another, abler, stronger, than myself, fresh to the task, with sharper tools than I have had. They may begin where I cease, and so toil on until at last some future toiler finishes the task and in the coming years humanity may stand upon the highest peak and there behold that glorious day when Justice linked with Liberty shall dwell in all the earth.

See also:

"15 Pictures of the Bar"

"14 Pictures of the Bench"

www.ingramcontent.com/pod-product-compliance
Lightning Source LLC
Chambersburg PA
CBHW070349220526
45467CB00001B/303